ONE-MINUTE PRAYERS™ for Women

TEXT BY HOPE LYDA

HARVEST HOUSE PUBLISHERS
EUGENE, OREGON

Cover by Franke Design and Illustration, Minneapolis, Minnesota

Cover photo © Trinette Reed/Photodisc Red/Getty Images

ONE-MINUTE PRAYERS is a series trademark of The Hawkins Children's LLC. Harvest House Publishers, Inc., is the exclusive licensee of the trademark ONE-MINUTE PRAYERS.

Portions of this book are taken from *One-Minute Prayers and One-Minute Prayers for Women.*

ONE-MINUTE PRAYERS™ FOR WOMEN GIFT EDITION
Copyright © 2004 by Hope Lyda
Published by Harvest House Publishers
Eugene, Oregon 97402
www.harvesthousepublishers.com

ISBN 978-0-7369-5476-1 (Milano Softone™)
ISBN 978-0-7369-2022-3 (Padded Hardcover)
ISBN 978-0-7369-3274-5 (eBook)

Printed in China

14 15 16 17 18 / RDS-CF / 26 25 24 23*

Contents

Beginning 5

Purpose. 7
Gifts 13
Direction. 19
Confidence 25
The Past 31
Preparation 37
Trust 43
Perspective 49
Dependence 55
Giving. 61
Letting Go 67
Prayer 71
Faithfulness. 77
Blessings 83
Opportunity 89
Grace. 95
Love 101
Seeking 107
Faith 113
The Future 119
Miracles. 125
Abundance 131
Provision 137

Renewal. 143
Plans 149
Grace. 155
Anticipation 161
Friendship. 167
Responsibility 173
Place 179
Longing. 185
Becoming 191
Intuition 197
Charity 203
Peace. 209
Affirmation 213
Truth. 219
Women 225
Relationships. 231
Freedom 237
Speaking Up 243
Holding On. 249
Stepping Out. 255
Asking God 261
Health 267
Dancing. 273

Tomorrow 279

You Began a Good Work

*In all my prayers for all of you, I always pray with
joy because of your partnership in the gospel from
the first day until now, being confident of this, that he
who began a good work in you will carry it on to
completion until the day of Christ Jesus.*

—PHILIPPIANS 1:4-6

When the bedside alarm sounds, concerns left over
from yesterday clutter my mind. A list of things to do
surfaces on my mental planner. Then come the choices.
What to wear? Which road will have less traffic this
morning? Tea, juice, coffee…decaf? latté? extra shot?

When did starting a day become so complicated?

Wait. My heart knows the answer to this one. I
recall a time when mornings began with one decision:
to spend time with You. Your Word smoothed the way.
The priorities for the day fell into place. The simple
choices did not distract me—I could step into work
of significance. Let me start this day over, Lord. I feel
Your presence pointing me in the right direction. I am
ready. Confident. For You began a good work in me,
and I will walk with You until it is completed.

Purpose

Exchanging My Plans for God's

Many are the plans in a man's heart, but it is the
LORD's purpose that prevails.

—PROVERBS 19:21

Lord, how many times have You heard me say, "So much to do, so little time"? When I catch myself repeating this mantra, it is followed by a shrug of resignation. Lord, is it the plight of humans to be so busy with plans for improvement, gain, success? My culture tells me it is so. God, shake the foundations of self-absorbed plans. Reveal to me the purpose You have for me, my time, my money, my work, my family, my today.

Take my tightly held heart. Reshape it. Let it expand to fit that place You have made for me in this world. Help me to not settle for a life of busyness that does not make room for what I should be doing. You have something far greater for me to grow into: Your purpose for my life.

My Purpose in Your Church

If you have any encouragement from being united with Christ, if any comfort from his love, if any fellowship with the Spirit, if any tenderness and compassion, then make my joy complete by being like-minded, having the same love, being one in spirit and purpose.

—PHILIPPIANS 2:1-2

Lord, help me to be like-minded with my community of fellowship. Guide me to compassion when in the presence of others' pain. Let me tend to people with the love You give. Empower me with a spirit of willingness to work with Your children.

I see a display of Your character wherever people are gathered, Lord. Our differences balance into wholeness through Your grace. It can be so difficult to look past the human idiosyncrasies. They distract us. They give us excuses to place people in categories or push them away. Let me see a person as a whole being. A physical, intellectual, and spiritual child of God. I pray that my actions will always help and not hinder the body of Christ's progression toward Your purpose.

How God Works

We know that in all things God works for the good of those who love him, who have been called according to his purpose.

—ROMANS 8:28

Lately, not many things seem to be working together for good, Lord. I am not complaining, just stating it like it is. But of course, I don't see as far down the road as You do…and perhaps a few of these situations just didn't work out in *my* favor. As I revisit the circumstances, maybe these moments were not about my personal success, but someone else's. Did I handle it well, Lord?

I pray for a sense of Your grand vision. Help me take every disappointing event, answer, and outcome and look at it from Your perspective. I may not see evidence of Your plan, so let me rest in my knowledge of Your love. Grant my heart peace when I am uncertain of the road I travel, Lord. I will keep moving, one foot in front of the other, because I have been called to good things.

What's Next?

The LORD will fulfill [his purpose] for me; your love, O LORD, endures forever—do not abandon the works of your hands.

—PSALM 138:8

Don't stop now, Lord. I am finally catching Your vision for my life. It has taken me a while, and I've had to walk through a lot of mistakes, but I am here and ready to receive Your purpose. What would You have me do next? Your patience over the years has shown me that You will not abandon the work You have begun. Lead me to the next step.

When I listen to others or even to my own negative thoughts, I am tempted to quit trying. Your love inspires me to keep going. And each time I move forward, my step is more steady. I am certain You will follow through. And I will follow Your example. So, what's next?

Gifts

According to God's Grace

We have different gifts, according to the grace given us. If a man's gift is prophesying, let him use it in proportion to his faith. If it is serving, let him serve; if it is teaching, let him teach; if it is encouraging, let him encourage; if it is contributing to the needs of others, let him give generously; if it is leadership, let him govern diligently; if it is showing mercy, let him do it cheerfully.

—ROMANS 12:6-8

Lord, which gifts have You given me? I do not want to waste a drop of my life by being blind to my potential in You. I seek a deeper understanding of Your Word. I want to comprehend how You manifest Yourself through spiritual gifts in Your children. I long to explore the lives of men and women in Scripture who followed You and who actively lived out their gifts.

According to the grace given me, I can live a fruitful life. I can share the amazing bounty of Your goodness with others. Help me to pay close attention to the work You are doing in my own heart. I want to see, understand, and cultivate the gifts that come from You.

Different Gifts of the Same Spirit

There are different kinds of gifts, but the same Spirit.
There are different kinds of service, but the same Lord.
There are different kinds of working, but the same
God works all of them in all men.

—1 CORINTHIANS 12:4-6

Lord, I stand in awe of Your love that is so great…so great that You have made each one of Your children unique, special, and miraculous. Our differences are not discerned just in physical characteristics or the language we speak, they are found in a kaleidoscope of gifts—all from the same Spirit.

Often my weakness is another's point of strength—my certainty, another's roadblock of doubt. You have created us to work together. Help me to acknowledge the gifts of others. I want to encourage the people I interact with to do and be their best…Your best. Guide my words, Lord, so that I express kindness and inspiration to my family, colleagues, and friends.

All I Have

As he looked up, Jesus saw the rich putting their gifts into the temple treasury. He also saw a poor widow put in two very small copper coins. "I tell you the truth," he said, "this poor widow has put in more than all the others. All these people gave their gifts out of their wealth; but she out of her poverty put in all she had to live on."

—LUKE 21:1-4

Forgive me for how tightly I hold on to the blessings in my life. I am too cautious in my giving. I even question how the one I give to will use my offering, as if that has anything to do with what giving is about. Along the way I have forgotten that giving is an act of sacrifice. It is an offering without strings, an expression of Your grace.

I don't want to hold back, Lord. I want to freely stretch out my hand to provide help, a blessing, a commitment to another. Prevent my heart from monitoring, counting, adjusting what I give. May I never keep track of such things. With Your gift of salvation as my only measure, I pray to give all I have in every moment.

These Are My Gifts

*On coming to the house, they saw the child with his
mother Mary, and they bowed down and worshiped
him. Then they opened their treasures and presented
him with gifts of gold and of incense and of myrrh.*

—MATTHEW 2:11

I open the treasure of my heart and look for gifts
to give You, my King. My offerings reflect the ways I
worship You each day. *Love* for my family. *Kindness* to
others. *Help* in the face of need. *Faith* in the future. *Trust*
through doubt. Lord, please accept these as responses
of my deep affection for You.

I bow down to You, Lord. Your grace transforms
my simple presents into precious metals and expensive
oils and perfume. Help me to watch for opportunities
to serve You by giving the gift of myself to others. And
let me recognize when I am receiving treasured pieces
of another's heart.

Direction

Following Directions

Walk in all the way that the LORD your God has commanded you, so that you may live and prosper and prolong your days in the land that you will possess.

—DEUTERONOMY 5:33

Lord, from Your vantage point, the charting of my daily course must look like a very unorganized spider's web. Here. There. Back again. How many days do I spend running in circles to keep up with the life I've created? Lead me to the life *You* planned for me. Unravel those strands of confusion and weave together a course that is of Your design.

This new vision for my life involves asking You for directions. Remind me of the beautiful pattern my steps can create when I seek Your help—when I feel lost *and* when I feel in control. Lord, give me the insight to follow Your commands. Guide me toward my true life.

The Guiding Force of Nature

He loads the clouds with moisture; he scatters his lightning through them. At his direction they swirl around over the face of the whole earth to do whatever he commands them.

—JOB 37:11-12

Lord, Your hand choreographs the dance of nature. You speak forth the rhythm of the ocean waves. Your word commands the clouds to rain on the thirsty land. The precise action and inaction of every element is under Your instruction. Why do I challenge the force of Your will in my life? I need only to witness the power of a stormy day or watch the sun dissolve into the horizon to know that You rule over all living things.

The beauty of creation can be mirrored in my own life. I must first give myself over to the dance that You choreograph. May I leap with full joy. Let my sweeping bow mimic Your grace. And as I stretch heavenward with open arms, may I be ready to receive the loving commands You rain down on me.

Moving into God's Love

May the Lord direct your hearts into God's love and
Christ's perseverance.

—2 THESSALONIANS 3:5

Lord, I confess I have been playing tug-of-war with
You. As You start to pull my heartstrings in one direction, I stubbornly resist. Goals and aims other than
Your best dazzle me with cheap imitations of love. I
avert my gaze for just a moment and lose sight of Your
plan. Instill in me a steadfast heart. Let me be single-
minded in my faith and trust.

Allow me to persevere in the direction You want
me to go. Let me not be tempted by false gods or
deceptive voices, which lead me astray. I should never
play games with my heart. After all, it belongs to You.
Take it now, Lord. I don't want to halt the beat of Your
love in my life.

A Parent's Instruction

My son, keep your father's commands and do not forsake your mother's teaching...When you walk, they will guide you.

—PROVERBS 6:20,22

"Don't touch the stove." "Look both ways." "Don't hit your sister." "Say you're sorry." Lord, the earliest instructions from my parents became lessons for my spiritual growth. The concept of cause and effect seeped past my resistance. Eventually I saw how parental guidance was about protection and concern.

Your commands reflect this truth from my childhood. I know that You guard my steps because You love me. I look to You before I proceed with a plan. I await Your approving nod before I make commitments and promises. Your Word lights my way even when I have run so far ahead that Your voice seems faint. Lord, may I always hear and heed Your directions. Guide me toward a righteous life.

Confidence

Certain of Your Protection

Have no fear of sudden disaster or of the ruin that overtakes the wicked, for the L ORD will be your confidence and will keep your foot from being snared.

—PROVERBS 3:25-26

The world feels out of control, God. I watch the news and turn away. But later, the fear of ruin, or violence, or disaster seeps into my soul. I am awakened by the pounding of my heart. While my daily routine finishes, I am anxious and unsettled. Lord, help me to place my confidence in You. I long for the peace You offer.

When I look to You, my spirit is soothed. Replace the list of dangers that runs through my mind with words of assurance. Let me witness Your hand on my life and in all circumstances. Turn my scattered worries into passages of prayer. When I see the world's pain, may I not use Your protection as a reason for isolation. Let me tap into Your love for empathy, compassion, and prayers of "Thy will be done."

Always My Hope

*You have been my hope, O Sovereign LORD, my con-
fidence since my youth.*

—PSALM 71:5

When I first came to know You personally, Lord, I stood so tall. I had unshakable faith in Your mightiness. When I am around a new believer, I feel that excitement once again. Restore this confidence, Lord. I will turn to the wisdom of Your Word and infuse my life with the security of Your promises.

Thank You, Lord, for the power You extend to me. The small windows of opportunity I once perceived are now wide-open doors. Everything is better when I stand in Your confidence. Fortify my life with the strength of Your plan. As I rise up to claim my hope in You, let me stand tall…just as I did in the youth of my faith.

He Hears Me

This is the confidence we have in approaching God: that if we ask anything according to his will, he hears us.

—1 JOHN 5:14

Lord, thank You for hearing me. Your ears are open to the musings of my heart, the longings of my soul, and the questions of my mind. There is nobody else in my life who promises to hear every part of me. Even in my most insecure moments, I utter words I know will reach Your heart. I dwell on worries my friends would not take seriously. I have fears that, brought up in daily conversation, would sound unreasonable. Yet, You listen.

It is a gift to be vulnerable with the Creator. You are my Master, yet I can come to You with the simplest needs or concerns. As Your child, I seek Your will and Your response. As my Father, You listen.

Without Shame

*Now, dear children, continue in him, so that when he
appears we may be confident and unashamed before
him at his coming.*

—1 JOHN 2:28

Purify me, Lord. My sinful ways build up pride and
lead me to worship idols of money, status, and success.
I have tried to hide my blemishes, my stains, but that
is a false life. I want the life You have laid out for me.
It is spotless and clean. It is a life to honor.

As You work out Your purpose in me, may I never
be boastful or arrogant. This detracts from You, the
Source of my confidence—and others will not understand that You are the Master of all that is good in my
life. Let my mouth be quick to praise Your grace, which
has removed my shame, healed my wounds, and made
me whole.

The Past

Communication Then and Now

In the past God spoke to our forefathers through the prophets at many times and in various ways, but in these last days he has spoken to us by his Son, whom he appointed heir of all things, and through whom he made the universe.

—HEBREWS 1:1-2

God, You had a communication plan in place at the inception of the universe. You knew Your children would need to hear Your voice. There are times I wish that Your prophets were still so easily recognized. Yet, would I even listen in this day and age? Likely, I'd bustle right past a proclaimed prophet in my hurry to catch the subway.

Lord, You know the shape of the past and the shape of things to come. You saw that the world would need a relationship with Your Son. A personal Savior to wake us up from our blurry, busy lives. I see You, God. I hear You. And I thank You for keeping the line of communication open through the power of Your Son.

Hope for the Future

Everything that was written in the past was written to teach us, so that through endurance and the encouragement of the Scriptures we might have hope.

—ROMANS 15:4

Lord, the wisdom of the lessons found in Your Word speaks to my life today. I thank You for the fresh hope that breathes through words scribed so many years ago. I am amazed how Scripture moves me. Some people try to cast it away as irrelevant, but they have not immersed themselves in Your truths.

You care so much for me, for all of Your children, that You created an unending source of encouragement and instruction. Help me to stay grounded in the teachings of the Bible, Lord. Show me the opportunities I have to live out the lessons of Scripture. I want to be an active student of Your love and Your ways.

The Rains Are Over

See! The winter is past; the rains are over and gone.
Flowers appear on the earth; the season of singing
has come.

—SONG OF SOLOMON 2:11-12

Days of hardship and pain have rained down in my past, Lord. There were storms that destroyed the foundations I had built. Floods swept away the hope I had placed in material things and in the strength I thought I saw in others. All that remained was the washed-out land of disappointment. But that was in the past. A time when I could not see a future.

Now the flowers sprout and shout from the earth. They sing a song of Your faithfulness. This is a new season for me, Lord. Past sorrows fade away and future hopes and dreams grow strong. You offer me this renewal every day, Lord. I am grateful for the rains, for they have prepared my soul to receive the blessings.

Moving On

Forget the former things; do not dwell on the past.
See, I am doing a new thing! Now it springs up; do
you not perceive it?

—ISAIAH 43:18-19

Free me from the past, Lord. I spend too much time there. Good times that have come and gone replay in my mind so often that I miss the wonder of today's joy. Cause me to return to the present, Lord. Draw my attention back to the life in front of me. My past has nothing to offer You or myself. But today…now…has so much to offer.

Give me a view of new wonders You are doing. I imagine they are brilliant happenings. Do not let my mind slip to the past, except to count the times You have blessed me. Then I must move on. My past serves my future…it is a foundation for all days that follow. Now, I must invest my time, my dreams, my prayers on the future You have carved out for me.

Preparation

Nourishment from Your Table

You prepare a table before me in the presence of my enemies.

—PSALM 23:5

When I face the opposition of the enemy, Lord, I can run to the table You are preparing for me. I am seated beside You—and I drink of Your wisdom, I eat of Your truth, and I am satisfied. I am saved here at Your table. My enemies and worries fade in the presence of my Host.

At each sitting I am nourished by Your banquet. When I leave the table to face my day, Your goodness follows me. I am filled with Your satisfying love. When I fear my enemies, I think of the security of Your eternal home. I shake my head in amazement that You promise to protect me, prepare the way for me, and reserve a place for me at the table of Your grace. You welcome me into Your presence, and I am blessed.

Prepared for Action

Prepare your minds for action; be self-controlled; set your hope fully on the grace to be given you when Jesus Christ is revealed.

—1 PETER 1:13

I try to exercise so that I am physically prepared for the demands of my daily life. But, Lord, I need help to prepare my mind and heart for the requirements of the spiritual life. I read Your Word and carry those lessons with me, but I admit I am still very weak. I face trials and still rely on my own strength rather than on the mightiness of Your power. I lose faith in Your ability to overcome my difficulties.

Lord, help me to truly be prepared. I need to go beyond head knowledge and claim a heart courage. Will I let myself fall back into Your arms when I feel weak, certain that You will catch me? Today, I am prepared to try.

A Room of My Own

In my Father's house are many rooms; if it were not so, I would have told you. I am going there to prepare a place for you. And if I go and prepare a place for you, I will come back and take you to be with me that you also may be where I am.

—JOHN 14:2-3

I remember the first time I had my own room. Even at a young age, I felt a sense of being cared for and provided for. Lord, I spent so much time preparing every detail in order to make it unquestionably mine. I think of this experience when I read Your promise to prepare a room for me. A place for me in heaven's glory.

When You take me home and show me this room, I am certain it will reflect how well You know my heart. The walls will be the shade of happiness. The fabrics will be woven with threads of loving memories. It will shimmer with Your splendor. I will run into it gladly, eager to be in Your presence forever. And I will know that the Master of the house prepared this room because I am unquestionably His.

A Ready Heart

Create in me a pure heart, O God, and renew a stead-fast spirit within me.

—PSALM 51:10

Just as You prepare a place for me, Lord, may I prepare a place for You. Create in me a clean heart that is pleasing to You. Make it a place that welcomes Your presence. God, I want a heart that clings tightly to Your promises. Let it beat strongly with Your purpose.

I want my soul to be a fortress that holds and protects Your Word within. Design a temple that is worthy to be called Your home. As I move through my days, I will think of the One who resides in me. Fill my heart with all that is pure and right so it will not be sacrificed to false gods but will be preserved and prepared for You alone.

Trust

Relying on You

*Pay attention and listen to the sayings of the wise;
apply your heart to what I teach, for it is pleasing
when you keep them in your heart and have all of
them ready on your lips. So that your trust may be
in the LORD, I teach you today, even you.*

—PROVERBS 22:17-19

Trusting in You changes everything, Lord. I will not
dwell on past failings, and I won't wager on things to
come. Because right now is my most important time
frame. Allow me to worship You better. Help me to
seek Your ways more earnestly. Let my thoughts and
my actions be pure in Your sight, Lord. I will heed the
lessons of the wise.

I see the day ahead and imagine ways to improve. I
will look for people who need encouragement, includ-
ing myself, and will recite words of Your faithfulness. I
will watch for the opportunities and unique moments
You offer that teach me more about You. Yes, I told
myself yesterday I was not worthy of Your love...but
the assurance of the sunrise this morning spoke of Your
grace. I trust You, Lord.

A Song to Sing

I trust in your unfailing love; my heart rejoices in your salvation. I will sing to the LORD, for he has been good to me.

—PSALM 13:5-6

God, You have been so good to me. I trust You and what You are doing in my life. Some days I clearly see Your love for me. I received a kind word at a time of sorrow. I was offered help when I was afraid to ask. And just when I thought I could not continue, I had a vision of what Your hand was doing in that very circumstance.

I could not navigate my days without trusting Your love and intent for good. I pray that my actions translate into lyrics for the world to hear. I want everyone to know the song of Your love and mercy. I lift up my voice to proclaim Your goodness. "I know a love that never fails me!" I cry out into a world of people who know only of broken love and misplaced trust. Thank You, Lord, for giving me a song to sing.

You Are Mine

I trust in you, O LORD; I say, "You are my God."

—PSALM 31:14

Lord, I want my lips to praise You in all situations. No matter the circumstances I am in, I want my first thoughts to be of praise, because I trust You with my life. May everything I do be a witness to this trust. When people around me attempt to fix my problems with temporal solutions, I will stand firm in my belief.

How often do I say, "You are my God"? Do my actions speak this? Do my relationships reflect this truth? I want every part of my life to resound with this statement. When Your peace replaces my worry, I want others to hear the reason. Let it be clear to people I meet that my trust is placed only in You. Help me to say it loudly, even in the silent moments that follow difficult times.

Entrusting a Soul

To you, O LORD, I lift up my soul; in you I trust, O my God. Do not let me be put to shame, nor let my enemies triumph over me.

—PSALM 25:1-2

In a moment of possible failure, Lord, am I trusting You to save me—or to save face for me? Help me lift up my soul without requirements and requests. I trust You to work out this situation for good, not evil. My humanity begs me to avoid humiliation at all costs, but I know I will be saved for different reasons: My weakness becomes evidence of Your strength. My destruction turns into a testimony of Your instruction and mercy.

Do not let me shame You, Lord. Let this moment shine light upon Your goodness. May it cast shadows on my need for recognition or reputation. Please accept this offering of my soul. There are no strings attached—only complete trust and gratitude come with this sacrifice.

Perspective

A Goal in View

A discerning man keeps wisdom in view, but a fool's eyes wander to the ends of the earth.

—PROVERBS 17:24

Okay, Lord, sometimes I become anxious about the plans I have under way. I start seeing the success that could follow. Or the different paths my life might take. What if this? What if that? I could end up here. Or there. Distracted by the possibilities, I step a bit to the side, turn without noticing, lose my balance. I become blind to Your priorities.

Lord, help me to keep Your wisdom in view. When my eyes start to scan the horizon of grand illusions, I lose perspective of what is right and reasonable. Guide me, Lord. Place Your hand on my shoulders and direct me. Give me discernment to keep my eyes trained on Your will.

Through a Worldly Lens

From now on we regard no one from a worldly point of view. Though we once regarded Christ in this way, we do so no longer. Therefore, if anyone is in Christ, he is a new creation; the old has gone, the new has come!

—2 CORINTHIANS 5:16-17

The eyes of a homeless man caught my attention today, Lord. They narrowed in the heat of the day and looked past me. I wondered when begging became necessary for him to survive. Did he have a family waiting for him at a shelter? Was his mother a worried, heartsick woman miles away? When was the last time he was comforted? I saw his thin, ragged figure through Your eyes, just for a moment, Lord, and I did not see a beggar—I saw a child of Your own.

A worldview through rose-colored glasses offers a selective look at pain, poverty, and need. Lord, I pray to adopt Your viewpoint. Let my heart have a vision of its own when I stand face-to-face with a child in need. The responsibility of a new vision scares me. But I stand before You, ragged and poor in spirit, and ask You to help me.

Looking Straight Ahead

Forgetting what is behind and straining toward what is ahead, I press on toward the goal to win the prize for which God has called me heavenward in Christ Jesus. All of us who are mature should take such a view of things. And if on some point you think differently, that too God will make clear to you.

—PHILIPPIANS 3:13-15

Lord, You know that thing I was worrying about last year? It has just surfaced again. It was a speck in the corner of my mind, and now it has taken over my field of vision. I fixate on it between phone calls and errands. Please help me strain toward what is ahead rather than dwell on what has ended. I want to press on toward the goal of a godly life.

Make it clear to me, Lord, when I am wasting precious time on matters of the past. You call me to go forward, to head toward eternity with assurance and purpose. Please, Lord, I want to exchange my life of limitation and blindness for Your ways of freedom and vision.

Examine Me

A man's ways are in full view of the LORD, and he examines all his paths.

—PROVERBS 5:21

It is painful for me to think about past mistakes. Because of the many sins that occupied my days and my ways, I missed opportunities. But that is not the difficult part...I know I have saddened Your heart, Lord. You watched me make those choices. You saw me choose pride over submission. I failed You and myself more times than I even know. But You know.

I have asked forgiveness of these past sins, and You forgave. Now, Lord, teach me Your way. Examine my new paths and find them holy and pleasing to You. When I get off course, pull me back to Your will. When I lose sight of my goal, show me Your perspective and lead me to examine my heart at every turn.

Dependence

Freedom Through Dependence

*If anyone acknowledges that Jesus is the Son of God,
God lives in him and he in God. And so we know
and rely on the love God has for us.*

—1 JOHN 4:15-16

Only You, Lord, offer me deep love. I dive in and feel Your presence all around me. We are a part of one another. Creator and creation. I am so blessed to have met and accepted the gift of Christ. This relationship is sufficient for all my needs. This love has covered my iniquities. Dependence has given me freedom and a path to eternity.

When I meet someone in pain, I want them to know Your love. How do they make it, if not with You? Even a life filled with blessings encounters stumbling blocks. Lord, next time I am hurt, broken, and weak, immerse me in the depths of Your mercy. As I surface and struggle for air, I depend on Your breath of life to fill my being.

I Trusted You Before
I Knew You

*From birth I have relied on you; you brought me
forth from my mother's womb. I will ever praise
you.*

—PSALM 71:6

Lord, You were there when I was formed in my
mother's womb. You knew my heart, my character,
my purpose as I was brought into the world. I was
so defenseless then, so vulnerable. I know Your hand
was upon my life for every minute. Even before I
had a personal relationship with You, I relied on You
completely.

Now I am so established in the world and can
appear strong and in control. But I confess I am as
vulnerable as the day I was born. I praise You for the
countless times You have protected me, saved me without my knowledge. O Lord, Your loving hand was and
will be with me every step of the way. I am so glad to
be Your child.

He Is My Mighty Rock

My salvation and my honor depend on God; he is
my mighty rock, my refuge.

—PSALM 62:7

Lord, You tower over my life. Your presence intimidates my enemies. You are my refuge during times of trouble. When I experience days of doubt, I climb onto Your rock of refuge. I stand against the wind and view my fretting from new heights. I see You crush my worries in the shadow of Your strength. I need not be afraid.

You are my safe place, Lord. I rise to sit on Your shoulders when I feel small. I lean against the weight of Your power and restore my strength. You are my security at all times. God, my life requires Your authority. I want You to reign over my days. Help me build a spirit of perseverance and a character of honor on the foundation of Your goodness.

See My Pain

Turn to me and be gracious to me, for I am lonely and afflicted. The troubles of my heart have multiplied; free me from my anguish. Look upon my affliction and my distress and take away all my sins.

—PSALM 25:16-18

Lord, see the depth of my pain. I am facing difficulties, and I feel alone as I seek solutions for my problems. Just as I put out one fire, I smell the smoke of another about to burst forth in flames. There has been so much. I don't know where to begin...except at the foot of Your cross. Free me, Lord. Take my anguish and my affliction and have mercy on my soul.

These problems that are surfacing—many are caused by bad decisions made in haste and without Your guidance. Forgive me, God. This isn't the first time I have been overwhelmed by trouble. Lord, give me strength. Turn to me and see the repentance in my eyes and heart.

Giving

The Reluctant Servant

The precepts of the LORD are right, giving joy to the heart.

—PSALM 19:8

Lord, when I was a child, I hated being told what to do. If asked to perform a chore, I resisted, found distractions, or muddled my way through it. Guidelines felt like punishment. I knew I was capable of doing the things that were asked of me—I just wanted to do them in my own way. I gave of myself in my own time frame.

How often do I resist Your precepts, Lord? I see the right way to give or serve, yet I fight it. I don't want to change my plans or be inconvenienced. I have had a reluctant heart, Lord, and I am sorry. Help me to follow Your commands with a giving spirit. I have asked many times before, but I still long to have a joyful heart that follows Your way.

Giving Light

God said, "Let there be lights in the expanse of the sky to separate the day from the night, and let them serve as signs to mark seasons and days and years, and let them be lights in the expanse of the sky to give light on the earth."

—GENESIS 1:14-15

Some people light up a room. I know Christians who reflect Your radiance everywhere they go, Lord. I want this kind of luster in my life. Show me how to give off a light that illuminates a moment. My faith needs to be polished to a sheen so that it sparkles and reflects Your face.

Guide me into action, Lord. Don't let me fall into a dark pit of apathy and make a home there. The further I distance myself from Your light, the less likely I am to be reignited in my passion for Your will. Most of all, I want my hope in You to give light to others. Help me shine, Lord.

Private Donations

When you give to the needy, do not let your left hand know what your right hand is doing, so that your giving may be in secret. Then your Father, who sees what is done in secret, will reward you.

—MATTHEW 6:3-4

It is hard to resist taking credit, Lord. Truth is, I am taking credit away from You every time I seek acknowledgment for giving my time, energy, or money. I feel so utterly human when I want affirmation. Isn't it enough to know that You see me and are pleased? Lord, help me to desire heaven's praise above all else. Guard me from a pretentious existence that feeds off recognition or success.

Any time I reach out to give to another, I am giving from Your source of plenty, not from any abundance I have created on my own. The credit is Yours to have. Humble my spirit so that the blessing of giving resides in my heart—in secret, under Your proud gaze. Pleasing You, Lord, is the only reward I desire.

Praise You

Speak to one another with psalms, hymns and spiritual songs. Sing and make music in your heart to the Lord, always giving thanks to God the Father for everything, in the name of our Lord Jesus Christ.

—EPHESIANS 5:19-20

Praise You. My spirits are lifted just saying that to You. So why am I quick to squelch the music of my soul? Some time ago, I told myself that songs and praises were shallow and emotional. Forgive me—Lord, I have forgotten that rejoicing is not frivolity—it is an offering to You.

I have held my tongue for too long. I will raise my hands to the sky. I will lift my voice to the heavens, and I will give You praise, Lord, for You are worthy. Hear my hymn of thanksgiving, Lord, for all You have done and are doing in my life. I will not silence my spirit in Your presence again.

Letting Go

I'm Pouting

These people have stubborn and rebellious hearts;
they have turned aside and gone away.

—JEREMIAH 5:23

I won't. I won't, Lord. Not just yet. I know I should let go of my recent behavior, but I just don't feel ready. You could make me, but You choose not to. Now, my choice is to pout for a while. My fingers are turning white as I grip this thing I will not release to You. I have a headache and really would rather rest. When did I become so difficult?

Sure, I'm shaking a little bit. My arms are growing weary. This is, after all, a heavy burden. I think I will set it down for a minute…just long enough to get some lunch. Without that huge anchor around my heart, I could take care of a few things after lunch. I sure feel better, Lord.

I'm picking it up again—this time to hand it over to You, Lord. I get it…when I let go of such things, I am free. I am choosing to be free, Lord. Thank You for waiting.

Come Near to Me, Lord

Submit yourselves, then, to God. Resist the devil, and he will flee from you. Come near to God and he will come near to you.

—JAMES 4:7-8

Submission is one of those concepts that bothers me, Lord. If You must know, it causes me to feel quite threatened. Help me to see the security that follows submission. I want to be under Your authority, Your control, Your cover of love. Forgive me for being tied to my identity as a self-made person. I have strived so long for control of my life that it feels unnatural to give it over to You.

Release me from my fear of submission, Lord. It has created a wall between us. Please come near to me. Empower me with the strength to resist the temptation to remain in control. I look forward to claiming the identity of a God-made person.

Prayer

Prayers for Healing

*This is what the L*ORD*, the God of your father David,
says: I have heard your prayer and seen your tears;
I will heal you.*

—2 KINGS 20:5

I weep in private, away from the well-meaning inquiries of friends. And You, Lord, see my tears. Awkward, shattered expressions of pain and confusion stumble from my lips, yet You heal the words. My prayer is whole when it falls upon Your heart. Your answer is complete: You love me. You see me. You will heal my brokenness.

It must be difficult to explain the ways of life and loss to Your children. When I ask "Why, Lord?" You do not turn away from me and my neediness. You hold me close and show Your heart. It is broken too—You have taken my pain. I watch Your tears fall and understand they have healed me.

Merciful Lord

The LORD has heard my cry for mercy; the LORD accepts my prayer.

—PSALM 6:9

I walked around numb and in denial for months, Lord. My façade was perfect. I didn't miss a beat at work. I stood in the grocery store express line and not one soul looked at me with pity. I encouraged a hurting friend with words that I myself could not yet accept about You: "You are a merciful Lord."

Then my heart spoke up. It sent out an SOS cry for mercy and compassion on my behalf. Lord, thank You for accepting this prayer. I could not gather the courage or energy to bring You my burdens. I was sick and tired of myself, but You raised me out of the trap of self-pity. I am a new creation. I accept the truth about You: You are merciful, Lord.

Prayer Song

By day the LORD directs his love, at night his song is with me—a prayer to the God of my life.

—PSALM 42:8

I sing to You, Lord. My joy, heartache, and thanksgiving create a symphony of emotion. In the solitude of nightfall, I cannot help but sing. I release the worries of my day to Your care. I trust You with my today and my tomorrow. My panic turns to peace as the first notes of praise drift heavenward.

Your concern touches me. Your voice blends with mine for a few sweet moments. You wrote this song to comfort me every night. You share it with me so I can come to You when the confines of words and dialogue stifle meaning. By day, Lord, guide me with Your love. By night, free me with Your melody. In every moment You are the God of my life.

True Devotion

Devote yourselves to prayer, being watchful and thankful.

—COLOSSIANS 4:2

God, can You work with me on my commitment issues? Build in me a desire to pray. I want to be a disciplined follower. Steady my spirit to stillness. Quiet and solitude prepare me for Your presence. Direct my eyes to be watching for Your answers, watching as my prayers are heard and responded to. I want to see and recognize Your work in my life.

Cause my faith to grow, Lord. Each day that I come to meet with You, may I know You better. Replace my ignorance with Your knowledge. Help me be strong in my commitment to You. Show me how to pray, Lord.

Faithfulness

I Am Your Child

The living, the living—they praise you, as I am doing today; fathers tell their children about your faithfulness.

—ISAIAH 38:19

Lord, I live today as Your child. I plan to focus on this identity. Undoubtedly I will be asking for guidance, messing things up, getting Your pristine plans dirty, and constantly asking, "Why? Why?" But You are used to the floundering of Your children. You are a patient parent. The lessons You have taught me in Your Word and through Your active love are helping me grow. I can see the person You want me to become.

Like a child, I will run in lots of different directions before asking the way. And by then, I will probably need to be carried. It is very exhausting being a child. But now, as You lift me up and comfort me with Your promise of love and grace, I settle down. To be wrapped in Your faithfulness is all I needed…I just didn't know how to get there. When I am done resting, will You tell me a story? I love the one about the day I became Your child.

Finding My Way Home

Love and faithfulness meet together; righteousness and peace kiss each other. Faithfulness springs forth from the earth, and righteousness looks down from heaven.

—PSALM 85:10-11

At the intersection of Your love and faithfulness, Lord, I have found my life. For years I have taken many detours. My soul longed for intrigue, so it turned down curious, narrow avenues; I found only pain and suffering. My spirit craved success and celebrity, so I ventured along the flashy main streets, only to find failure and isolation.

Then I stopped following my "wants" and listened to my heart. My pace quickened as I caught a glimpse of the crossroads ahead. You waited patiently for me on the corner. I didn't ask what it was You were promising or how long it would last. I could see home in Your eyes, and it went on forever.

Flawless and Faithful

*O Lord, you are my God; I will exalt you and praise
your name, for in perfect faithfulness you have done
marvelous things, things planned long ago.*

—ISAIAH 25:1

I did not give You much to work with early on in
my life, Lord. What a sight I was back then. Rumpled,
tough, stubborn, and ignorant. "Just try to do something with this!" I challenged You on a particularly
bad day. I was acting out the courage found in movie
heroes, but my heart was really pleading with You,
"*Please*—do something with my life."

You answered this cry for help because You knew
I would someday step into Your faithfulness and be
transformed into a shining, perfect child of God. You
turned my spirit of spite into a heart of praise. Praise
You, Lord. Long ago You planned such marvelous
things for my life. I cannot wait to see where Your
faithfulness will lead.

Your Creation Endures

Your faithfulness continues through all generations;
you established the earth, and it endures.

—PSALM 119:90

Beneath my feet is proof of Your commitment, Lord. You established the earth and set it in motion to serve Your children and Your greater purpose. Your creation speaks of Your enduring faithfulness. God, the lineage of just one family has countless testimonies of Your limitless love.

I pray that I will carry on stories of Your holiness to others in my family. Let my praises spread to those in my spiritual family. May I then speak of Your goodness to those who do not yet know You. May I always be a faithful child who models the faithfulness of my Father.

Blessings

Receiving God's Blessing

May God give you of heaven's dew and of earth's richness—an abundance of grain and new wine.

—GENESIS 27:28

I have had my share of goodness, Lord. I need only to look at my immediate surroundings and the people in my life to see how richly I have been blessed. Why do I pay such close attention to the imperfections of my life? *My job could be more important. My family could be a bit more agreeable. My body could be in better shape, like the woman on that television show. My car could be newer and have all of those extras I saw on the commercials that interrupted that television show.* You see how my mind starts to destroy all the blessings?

Lord, open my eyes to the good in all situations. Let the times of poverty I experience cause me to embrace the richness of Your bounty. Help me to be aware of the manna that falls from heaven and lands in my life.

Satisfied by Grace

From the fullness of his grace we have all received one blessing after another.

—JOHN 1:16

I look at the life You have given me, Lord, and I see great blessings. You have provided for my needs. Your grace has allowed me to reach goals. There is so much more I want to do, but I have learned to wait on Your timing. There is an order to godly things. When I let Your priorities guide my journey, blessings build upon blessings.

Hold me back when I try to force advancement, Lord. I don't want anything in my life, even if it resembles success, if it is not from You. I pray for discernment to know the difference between aspirations fabricated by my heart and those born of Your will. Free me from thoughts of envy, judgment, and greed. I want to be satisfied by Your grace alone.

Inherit a Blessing

Do not repay evil with evil or insult with insult, but with blessing, because to this you were called so that you may inherit a blessing.

—1 PETER 3:9

Lord, I am more likely to hold a grudge than release a blessing when someone has hurt me. My reaction to conflict reveals how desperately I need Your forgiveness to flow through me. Heal me from the anger that rises so quickly. I want to reflect Your image to others, even those who are working against me.

Let me ponder Your holiness before facing a potentially difficult encounter or situation. I want to arm myself with Your Word, Your strength, and Your compassion so I can honor Your name with my actions. I will inherit a blessing by spreading the legacy of Your love.

Find Me Righteous

*Surely, O L*ORD*, you bless the righteous; you surround them with your favor as with a shield.*

—PSALM 5:12

Search my heart, O Lord. May You find it righteous and pure. I long for joy in my life. This season of hardship has tempted me to question how Your blessings are given. What have I done to deserve this pain? But my heart knows I am forgiven—Your mercy covers my sins. How can I use this time to draw closer to You rather than challenge Your mercy?

What do You want me to learn from my life today? Alleviate my confusion. Pierce my heart with Your love. Encourage me with the security of believing friends. Saturate my days with evidence of blessings yet to come. Surround me with Your favor. Protect my fragile heart.

Opportunity

Embracing the Unknown

*Show me your ways, O LORD, teach me your paths;
guide me in your truth and teach me, for you are
God my Savior, and my hope is in you all day
long.*

—PSALM 25:4-5

Father in heaven, You see all that takes place in my
life. Knowing this gives me peace as I face transition. I
exchange my uncertainty for Your promise of security.
Open my eyes to the wonders of every turn, tangent,
and seeming detour I encounter. I don't want to miss a
miracle by starting a new journey diminished by regret,
pride, or misplaced longing. I want to long for You. For
the path You carve out for me.

Remove the blinders from my physical and spiritual
eyes, Lord. I want to see the beauty of the landscape
You have built around me. And I want to savor the
opportunity that rests on the horizon. As I face a new
direction, this time my heart flutters with excitement
and not with worry. I am eager to see what You have
in store for me. I accept Your provision, Lord.

Doing Good

As we have opportunity, let us do good to all people, especially to those who belong to the family of believers.

—GALATIANS 6:10

Where can I do the most good, Lord? Direct me. Guide me to the people You want me to serve. I used to give only to random causes and organizations. My offering at church became my "I gave at the office" excuse when other needs arose. Then, Lord, You allowed me to personally experience small kindnesses. I came to understand how the little matters mean the most. Create a clean motive in my heart, God. May I do good purely to honor You, and not my own reputation.

Help me reach out and establish real relationships. Even if my encounter with a person is for one day, one hour, one smile, this is my opportunity to serve You. I will wait, watch, and act on these opportunities.

Choosing Peace

If it is possible, as far as it depends on you, live at peace with everyone.

—ROMANS 12:18

Lord, I long for Your peace in my soul. I wish to draw it in and release it to others. Where I have a chance to act out Your peace, please let me be strong and brave. Conflict is easier sometimes. It allows me to build barriers between me and another, or between me and the right way. But there is little comfort when I stand alone, indignant on one side of the wall.

May I meditate on Your Word so that it rises to my mind in place of angry and defensive language. Peace flows from You and into my life. I know its power to change behavior and remove blindness. Grant me the opportunity to share this gift.

Opportunity of a Lifetime

*He replied, "You are talking like a foolish woman.
Shall we accept good from God, and not trouble?"*

—JOB 2:10

When my timeline, career, family life, and spiritual
walk are going as planned, I accept Your ways, Lord. I
rest in how rewarding my faith can be. But when I face
hardship, I assume You have left me or have caused
me pain. I know this is not truth. You do not give us
more than we are able to bear. God, help me sense Your
active presence. Teach me Your mercy so that I never
question it again. Give my heart a measure of promise
to keep me going.

Plant in me a trust that will take firm root. Help
me recall the previous times when difficulties turned
into lessons, strength, and even blessing. May I see
every obstacle as an opportunity to accept *all* that You
have for me.

Grace

Living Grace

Each one should use whatever gift he has received to serve others, faithfully administering God's grace in its various forms.

—1 PETER 4:10

"God works in mysterious ways." People say that. I say that. But as I examine life, Lord, I see You also work in practical, concrete, anything-but-mystical ways. A friend comforted me during a recent stretch of bad days. A stranger helped me change a flat tire on the freeway during rush hour. The clerk at the video store found and returned my lost wallet. Everyday happenings, upon observation, are really vignettes of Your grace.

People sharing their gifts of empathy, kindness, and honesty express Your love. Lord, when I feel that same tug on my heart, let me be faithful in following through with Your direction. I see how honoring the gifts You have graciously given is really about making connections with Your other children. Your mercy is found in the most mundane situations, and when we least expect it. Help me to watch for Your living grace.

Rich with Redemption

In him we have redemption through his blood, the forgiveness of sins, in accordance with the riches of God's grace that he lavished on us with all wisdom and understanding.

—EPHESIANS 1:7-8

Keep me from being spiritually poor, Lord. In the material realm, I want for nothing. I have food to eat and a roof over my head. I have the means to care for my family. I even have tasted the luxury of abundance. But it takes wisdom to amass spiritual riches. Lead me to understand the treasures of salvation.

Your love inspires and satisfies me, Lord. I have been redeemed through the sacrifice of Christ. Your grace leads to spiritual riches. It multiplies to cover every one of my iniquities. My soul was purchased for a price, and it has made me a wealthy child of God.

I Work So Hard

It is by grace you have been saved, through faith—and this not from yourselves, it is the gift of God—not by works, so that no one can boast. For we are God's workmanship, created in Christ Jesus to do good works, which God prepared in advance for us to do.

—EPHESIANS 2:8-10

I work so industriously, God. There is sweat on my brow as I survey the fruits of my labor. Signs of my hard work are everywhere. I dedicate the work of my hands to You. And yet, I resist the one thing You call me to do right now—fall to my knees and accept Your grace. Why is that so difficult for me, Lord?

Soften my heart to receive Your saving grace. Eliminate in me the need to earn Your love. You freely give Your grace so I can focus on doing the good works You have prepared for me. Grant me a deeper understanding of Your provision. And receive my humble spirit as I rest in Your mercy.

Approaching the Throne

Let us...approach the throne of grace with confidence, so that we may receive mercy and find grace to help us in our time of need.

—HEBREWS 4:16

I am stepping out in faith, Lord. I hold my hands out to You with expectation. Pour Your grace over me. Let it cover me, fill me, and then overflow from me. I need You today, Lord, more than ever before. I walked around for months in false confidence based on my ability. It fell apart. As soon as one stone was cast at my façade, I came crumbling down in fragments of dust and pride.

Breathe Your mercy into my soul. Let my body depend on it more than oxygen. Rebuild my life according to Your plan. Only then can I return to You with confidence to ask for help, ask for Your grace, ask to be whole.

Love

Love One Another

Let no debt remain outstanding, except the continuing debt to love one another, for he who loves his fellowman has fulfilled the law.

—ROMANS 13:8

God, I pray for renewal in my relationships with family and friends. My heartstrings are tied to so many people that I sometimes lose sight of the uniqueness and privilege of each individual relationship. Guide my thoughts and my prayers so that I would be discerning the needs of those You have brought into my life. May I see how each friend and family member is a part of the body of Christ.

When I need encouragement and laughter, draw me to those who offer such nourishment. I thank You for the people in my life who bring comfort, who pray for me, and who are examples of Your love. Some connections are fragile and tenuous, others are deeply rooted and mighty; I pray for wisdom to know how to nurture each one.

All My Heart

*Hear, O Israel: The L*ORD *our God, the L*ORD *is one.*
*Love the L*ORD *your God with all your heart and with*
all your soul and with all your strength.

—DEUTERONOMY 6:4-5

Lord, give me the capacity to love fully, completely. I hold back. I stay aloof on matters of the heart when I should be diving in headfirst. When I look at the cross, I know You have shown me the deepest depths of mercy. Sacrifice. Forgiveness. Salvation. Help me embrace this model of perfect love and live it each day.

Maybe because I know I can never repay You for Your mercy, I resist trying to return Your love. Please accept my offering of love. It will not be all You deserve, but I will try. Your Word and Your living example inspire me to greater passion. I want to be consumed by my love for You, Lord, until You possess all of my heart and soul.

Better than Life

Because your love is better than life, my lips will glorify you.

—PSALM 63:3

My favorite things in life are examples of Your perfect beauty. A sky so blue it reflects peace. Friendships so strong they mirror Your faithfulness. Happiness so deep it encompasses Your joy. I cannot separate You from these miracles of life, because You are at the core of them. And as much as I cherish these gifts, I know Your love for me and for Your creation is even more vibrant.

Lord, I praise Your presence in every remarkable thing. Your radiance illuminates the miraculous in each moment. May I sing Your praises all the day long. May my lips glorify You because there is nothing better than Your love.

You Heard Me

I love the LORD, for he heard my voice; he heard my cry for mercy. Because he turned his ear to me, I will call on him as long as I live.

—PSALM 116:1-2

I don't need to take anyone's word for it, Lord—I know You answer prayer. I love to hear of others who have called out to You, and how You soothed their pain...but I don't need those examples for assurance. I know of Your goodness and mercy. I have been the one to call out in desperation. At times when I felt the most undeserving of Your attention, You turned Your ear to me and were faithful.

You reach out to me in my darkest hour and You hold me, comfort me, and see my sorrow. Your compassion is a balm for my soul. My tears fall freely at the thought of Your unconditional love. I don't need to be convinced of Your mercy, because when I cried out to You, my Lord, You heard me.

Seeking

Heart and Soul

Now devote your heart and soul to seeking the LORD your God.

—1 CHRONICLES 22:19

Lord, do I pursue You as I should? I have had hobbies take over my life. Do I give You the same attention? I spend countless hours perusing bookstores and immersing myself in the riches of the written word. When was the last time I gave my spiritual quest the same amount of energy? It's been a while.

I realize I have become lax in my pursuit of You, Lord. You and my faith should occupy my mind more than a part-time interest. Infuse my soul with a desire to pursue You wholly. Completely. I want to know everything about You. I hunger for Your Word. I devote my heart and soul to seeking You and Your will for my life.

Name Above All Names

Those who know your name will trust in you, for you, LORD, have never forsaken those who seek you.

—PSALM 9:10

I know Your name so well, Lord. I whisper it in times of sorrow. I hold it close when entering a place of fear. I shout its praise during times of celebration. You have carved it on my heart so that I will never forget the Creator of my soul. I do not go anywhere without being covered by Your name, for it is powerful.

When I experience doubt, Lord, remind me that "he will be called Wonderful Counselor, Mighty God, Everlasting Father, Prince of Peace." You are all these things to me, Lord. Let me never forget to call on You, the One who does not forsake me but leads me to higher places.

Thoughts of God

In his pride the wicked does not seek him; in all his thoughts there is no room for God.

—PSALM 10:4

Lord, reveal to me where I am prideful. What causes me to stumble while trying to do Your will? Obstacles that grow in size and threaten to become permanent in my life hinder my view of Your face. Even though it will be painful, please remove these barriers to a holy life.

Heal me from blindness caused by too much self-focus. When my eyes turn only toward my own life, I lose sight of the future You have for me. My worries weigh me down and immobilize me when I should be seeking Your freedom. Lord, please take away my selfish thoughts. They crowd out Your voice, the voice that gives me purpose.

Justice for All

Many seek an audience with a ruler, but it is from the LORD *that man gets justice.*

—PROVERBS 29:26

I want to be heard, Lord. I always want to tell my side of a situation so an authority can vindicate me. But it is You, Lord, who should receive my call for justice. You are the judge of my soul and my life—why should I seek out any other rulers? In the same way, help me to resist determining the fate of another. It is not my right to stand in Your place.

Lord, guide me in Your ways when there is conflict. Fill me with wisdom, honesty, and courage, and let me rely on their strength if I am accused. Keep me blameless so no harm is brought to Your name. Guard my heart from resentment if I am not treated fairly. May I live out forgiveness and faith, anticipating the justice of love I will receive when in Your presence.

Faith

Restored by Faith

He touched their eyes and said, "According to your faith will it be done to you"; and their sight was restored.

—MATTHEW 9:29-30

Heal me, Lord, from the inside out. My spirit is sick from worry and stress. Create a healthy soul inside this temple. I have neglected to nourish my spirit—show me the way back. Wounds ignored for too long need Your healing touch. Remove scars that remind me of old but not forgotten hurts. I trust You to mend my brokenness.

Let me have the same belief when I need physical healing. I know You hear and answer these prayers. Help me to understand that I do *not* understand the vast number of ways in which You heal. My human eyes can be blind to Your acts of mercy. Restore my sight, Lord. Let me feel Your touch and hear You say, "According to your faith will it be done to you."

Facing the Storm

Without warning, a furious storm came up on the lake, so that the waves swept over the boat. But Jesus was sleeping. The disciples went and woke him, saying, "Lord, save us! We're going to drown!" He replied, "You of little faith, why are you so afraid?" Then he got up and rebuked the winds and the waves, and it was completely calm.

—MATTHEW 8:24-26

Craziness consumes me, Lord. Beneath the confidence I show the world, God, You know an ocean of fear rocks and swells. I feel it when I spend a few minutes in silence. That is why I avoid quiet time with You. I'm afraid to face the storm.

God, I am just like the disciples who followed You and listened to Your many explanations of what it means to believe. I have heard Your parables and witnessed Your faithfulness, yet I cry, "Save me," with little faith. Pull my gaze to Your eyes. Do not let me look at the waves about to crash into my ordered world. When the winds die down and I face You on the calm waters, I want to be found standing as a faithful servant.

Nothing Is Impossible

"I tell you the truth, if you have faith as small as a mustard seed, you can say to this mountain, 'Move from here to there' and it will move. Nothing will be impossible for you."

—MATTHEW 17:20

All-powerful Lord, Your might is a part of my life. The incredibleness of this truth is my reason for often neglecting Your resource. How can it be possible that You allow Your children such strength? What an awesome God You are. History shows us that kings of men often strip their followers of hope. But You clothe those in Your kingdom with possibility.

Show me what faith, even the smallest faith, can accomplish, Lord. Next time I face a mountain on my spiritual journey, I will not ask if You will help me to the top. Instead, I will draw forth a faith that requires the obstacle be moved altogether.

Promises to Others

*Have we not all one Father? Did not one God create
us? Why do we profane the covenant of our fathers
by breaking faith with one another?*

—MALACHI 2:10

I want to be a keeper of promises. Lord, lead me to
make only commitments I am strong enough to fulfill.
Good intentions cause me to step up to meet many
needs. But I have discovered something…I am not a
good judge of time and responsibility. Forgive me for
letting down even one other person. Free in Your mercy,
I do not have to live a life buried in guilt—but I do
desire to be honorable before others and You.

Guard me from becoming overconfident and inde-
pendent. That is when I take on too many demands.
Protect me from breaking bread with a friend one day,
then breaking faith with them on another. Bless me with
a heart whose generosity is followed by perseverance
and commitment.

The Future

Your Perfect Will

Do not conform any longer to the pattern of this world, but be transformed by the renewing of your mind. Then you will be able to test and approve what God's will is—his good, pleasing and perfect will.

—ROMANS 12:2

So many choices and decisions seem to fill my world, Lord. I pray to rest in Your will and Your way so that I do not lose sight of my future as a child of God. My work can consume me, and my worries about material things can undermine the blessings. Change my heart, Lord. Let the matters of eternal importance become my priority list.

Oh, how I crave a life of significance. But even as I pray, a flood of insecurities can fill me, and I have no room left for the purpose You wish to pour into my cup. Let me not be anxious to fill my life with clutter and trivial distractions, Lord. Let my life, my heart, my soul be vessels that await the flow of Your Spirit.

Release Me from Worry

Who of you by worrying can add a single hour to his life? Since you cannot do this very little thing, why do you worry about the rest?

—LUKE 12:25-26

Lord, You are my source of strength in all things. How do I forget that Your mighty hand is placed upon my life? Today, I give over to You the many things that occupy my mind and my heart. Help me to release my worries to You as they take hold of me. These anxieties keep me from embracing the life You have planned for me. Your mercy surrounds me with comfort. Your love is my source of strength, and it is my future.

Meet me today, Lord. Here in this moment. In the midst of the troubles that weigh me down. Sometimes it is difficult for me to ask for help. To admit to weakness. But my soul is weary, and I want to give my burdens over to You. You are a mighty, faithful God. Thank You, Lord, for hearing my prayers today and every day. My spirit is buoyed as my prayers are spoken. I love You, Lord.

Hope and a Future

"I know the plans I have for you," declares the LORD, "plans to prosper you and not to harm you, plans to give you hope and a future."

—JEREMIAH 29:11

My to-do lists and the task reminders that pop up on my computer screen reflect a bit of my nature. Lord, I like to know what will occur and how it will take place. No surprises for me, please. I equate the unknown with potential problems. Cure me, Lord, of such a pessimistic view of my future. I have hope…I just want control too. It is so very shortsighted of me to have such little trust in You, the Creator of the world and of my life.

Reach out and still my active, worried mind so it receives and accepts Your Word. You have plans to prosper me and not to harm me. Replace my anticipation of complications with assurance of security. May I start and end my to-do lists with prayers of thanksgiving.

Self-Talk

I am convinced that neither death nor life, neither angels nor demons, neither the present nor the future, nor any powers, neither height nor depth, nor anything else in all creation, will be able to separate us from the love of God that is in Christ Jesus our Lord.

—ROMANS 8:38-39

If I could have a conference call with my past self, present self, and future self, I believe I would discover one truth: Your love has always been with me. The voices of my self over the course of my life would share stories about testing Your commitment. I tried to measure Your love by running far from heaven's reach. I stretched Your love by pushing the boundaries. I shoved away Your love when my doubt tried to poke holes in Your truth.

And Your love remained.

I have many questions about my future, but after listening to the course of my life, one thing is certain—my heart will never be separated from the love of its Creator.

Miracles

Something Remarkable

Everyone was amazed and gave praise to God. They were filled with awe and said, "We have seen remarkable things today."

—LUKE 5:26

Lord, I confess I have been thinking about how unremarkable my life is. I wake up, I go to work, I try to be a good friend and a loving member of my family, but nothing extraordinary takes place. It is just me, moving through the daily necessities.

Lord, forgive me…I have forgotten how remarkable it is to breathe in and out, to be alive. Somehow I have ignored the privilege of true joy. And how many times have I been amazed by Your compassionate covering of my hurts? Each day that I move deeper into the future You have planned for me is a miracle of renewal. Praise You, Lord, for You are doing remarkable things in my life today. Sometimes I just need to be reminded.

Tell the World

"Everybody living in Jerusalem knows they have done an outstanding miracle, and we cannot deny it. But to stop this thing from spreading any further among the people, we must warn these men to speak no longer to anyone in this name."

—ACTS 4:16-17

So many around the world and throughout history have tried to silence Your name, Lord. But Your name and the gospel of salvation continue to reach across continents and into the hearts of people. I think of Your disciples, who were asked not to discuss the miracles performed through Your power. They were warned and threatened, yet they said they could not help speaking about all they had seen and heard. They faced risk and still remained true to You.

I thank You for freedom to share my faith. I can talk about the miraculous love I have experienced. Encourage me to use this blessing. Give me the courage to be a disciple who refuses to silence the sound of a miracle.

Because I Believe

Does God give you his Spirit and work miracles among you because you observe the law, or because you believe what you heard?

—GALATIANS 3:5

Lord, I believe You and I believe in You. This is my foundation as I read about Your miracles in Scripture. But the power behind such wonders is more than people of that day or our day can fathom. God, I acknowledge that I too want to place the works of Your hand up against the laws of man and nature and scrutinize them. Just a little.

Even today, I read of miraculous moments that are evidence of Your work—and I must first fight the urge to see if there is another explanation. Help me to believe what I hear and read. Give me discernment in such matters so I can fully embrace the signs of Your Spirit at work today.

Climate Control

He did not do many miracles there because of their lack of faith.

—MATTHEW 13:58

Lord, heal me from my disbelief. A climate of faith welcomes Your wonders. Has my lack of faith kept You from performing a miracle in my life? It is hard for me not to be cynical sometimes. I start by being frustrated about the condition of the world, my city, my family, or my self—then, I let these feelings bleed over into my faith. Do not let me taint my spirit any further, Lord.

Restore to me a faithful heart, Lord. Lead me to people who are encouragers and who counter the apathy that builds up in my daily life. I want to be overflowing with faith. I want to be ready to receive a miracle.

Abundance

Telling of Your Goodness

*They will tell of the power of your awesome works,
and I will proclaim your great deeds. They will
celebrate your abundant goodness and joyfully sing
of your righteousness.*

—PSALM 145:6-7

Lord, Your awesome works are everywhere. Goodness flows through many channels but comes from You alone. Strengthen my spirit so I will be bold when speaking of Your greatness. I can be shy about sharing You. Or sometimes it seems self-righteous of me to mention my faith. Lord, guide my heart to speak truth at all times. Let my words never be forced, but freeflowing from You, the Source of all goodness.

When I share about You with others, help them discover and celebrate Your abundant love and mercy. Give me a voice to sing of Your righteousness. Direct my path toward those who need to hear the good news. And when I forget it in my own life, remind me of this prayer and the praises I feel in my heart today.

With or Without

I know what it is to be in need, and I know what it is to have plenty. I have learned the secret of being content in any and every situation, whether well fed or hungry, whether living in plenty or in want. I can do everything through him who gives me strength.

—PHILIPPIANS 4:12-13

Lord, Your hand has guided me through times of want and times of plenty. I thank You for being my Source of strength and guidance. When I hungered for more and thirsted for opportunity, I followed Your way to brighter days. You guided me through years of abundance so that I could be a devoted steward of my blessings. My status in the world's eyes might change, but my relationship with You remains the same.

Teach me about contentment, Lord. When I have material wealth, may I still long for spiritual direction and nourishment. As I experience difficulties, lead my thoughts and prayers to You for direction and hope. I can do all things and survive all circumstances through Your strength.

Dream-Come-True

*He who works his land will have abundant food, but
he who chases fantasies lacks judgment.*

—PROVERBS 12:11

I have a hard time staying focused. Any bit of
dazzle catches my eye. When someone passes by who
is living the life I covet, I turn my head and watch them
walk away. Fix my mind on the work in front of me,
Lord. Return my attention and intentions to the many
important and wonderful pieces of my life.

When my head is in the clouds, dreaming of what
I want or think I need, pull me back into the abundant
day You have given me. I have family, friends, health,
and You. The tasks I face today will reap rewards that
are real—not just material pleasures, but emotional
treasures like satisfaction, fulfillment, contribution,
meaning, and purpose. I'll keep dreaming, Lord, but
I will ground my days in my dream-come-true: Your
unconditional love.

What's Mine Is Yours

O Lord our God, as for all this abundance that we have provided for building you a temple for your Holy Name, it comes from your hand, and all of it belongs to you.

—1 CHRONICLES 29:16

Everything I create, Lord, is Your creation. My best ideas are manna from heaven. The life I am building is a temple that belongs to You. May I give You all and understand that You are the Source of every good thing I have. When I sit back and look fondly at my family, I know they are a gift from You.

Free me from the burden of owning things, Lord. I will keep up my responsibilities and tend to whatever is in my care, but release me from the desire to claim things as my own: *I want. I need. I must have.* This train of thought is getting old. I want to rest in knowing You own all things. Blessings come from Your hand, and that is where I in turn will place them.

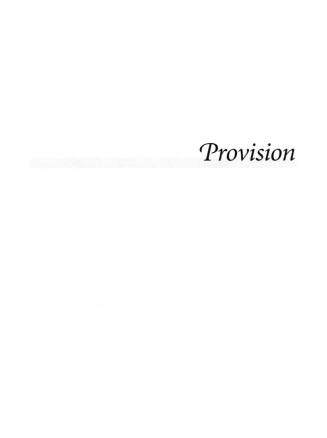

Provision

Daily Bread

Give us today our daily bread.

—MATTHEW 6:11

Lord, I give You my entire day. I humbly lift up the sacrifice of my daily living to be used to Your glory. This empty vessel will be filled with strength, courage, hope, and blessing…Your provision flows like living water, and it is plentiful. May others see that You are the One who gives me life and who provides for my daily needs. You, who are the bread of life, do not let any one of Your children go hungry.

Where there was nothing in my life, there is now a bounty of goodness. Dry land has turned to thriving pastures. And when I grow hard toward such blessing and cry out for more in the presence of so much, remind me that the daily bread You give *is* enough. Let my heart open up to Your gracious gifts. And may each day I give to You be worthy in Your sight.

Refreshment

You gave abundant showers, O God; you refreshed your weary inheritance. Your people settled in it, and from your bounty, O God, you provided for the poor.

—PSALM 68:9-10

I grow weary on my journey sometimes. You have carried me often, Lord. I have felt used and useless when going through a rough spot—a dry existence that lacks nourishment and substance. Anything I try to grow just withers and blows away toward the horizon…far away from me.

I look back on these times of my journey. You have sent showers of refreshment in many ways—opportunities appeared when I doubted their existence, kindness humbled me and my bad attitude, and abundant love flooded through me. Your provision has brought me back to life. My path continues, and I am no longer afraid of the droughts I may face along the way.

Learning to Share

*Command those who are rich in this present world
not to be arrogant nor to put their hope in wealth,
which is so uncertain, but to put their hope in God,
who richly provides us with everything for our enjoyment. Command them to do good, to be rich in good
deeds, and to be generous and willing to share.*

—1 TIMOTHY 6:17-18

Who can follow the stock market? I get really
confused. I feel left behind in the race for wealth.
Keeping up with the Joneses isn't the standard
anymore—everyone wants to keep up with movie
stars and computer moguls. Lord, help me out of this
cycle of depravity. Make me rich in my love for others.
Direct my longings back to You and Your wealth of
spiritual abundance.

Lord, I have sufficient...no, *ample* wealth. Teach me
the ways of a good steward and a faithful servant. Let
my money follow my heart for You. Use my resources
to bring blessing to others. You richly provide, Lord—I
am investing in Your hope.

What a Life Produces

*Our people must learn to devote themselves to doing
what is good, in order that they may provide for daily
necessities and not live unproductive lives.*

—TITUS 3:14

I have been devoted to a number of things over the
years. Sadly, a few of them were passing fancies, trendy
needs. And I learned a lot from their demise. Lord, You
are my one true devotion. Help me take the next step
after loving You: following You.

Cultivate in me a character of decency. Let me work
hard and carry out deeds of kindness. May Your seeds
of grace fall on fertile soil in my heart so a harvest of
honor is later reaped. I pray that I would turn Your
provision into continuous seasons of productive goodness. I want to live a life pleasing to You and beneficial
to others. Direct me in Your ways and keep my spirit
burning with devotion.

Renewal

Running on Low

You were wearied by all your ways, but you would not say, "It is hopeless." You found renewal of your strength, and so you did not faint.

—ISAIAH 57:10

I always dreamed of being a respected, productive woman with many responsibilities. But my imaginings shone the spotlight on a false picture of the calm, collected, posed and poised, well-dressed version of myself. But in reality, Lord, the tasks and commitments involved in being a successful woman can become tedious. I grow weary.

When I am running on low, I run to the Most High. Lord, refresh my spirit today. Infuse my body and soul with Your limitless strength and might. When my legs are about to buckle from the weight of real and perceived obligations, remind me to embrace the plan You have for my life. I need to give You what is on my plate every day. Only then will my steps be strong enough to carry me on the right path.

Inside Out

Create in me a pure heart, O God, and renew a steadfast spirit within me.

—PSALM 51:10

Forgive me, God. I give my heart away too easily to things of the world. It is smudged from such insincerity. It has cracks from moments of mishandling. Cleanse my heart, Lord. I want it to be shiny enough to reflect Your goodness. Mend the broken places, if You will. I long to feel the beating of a whole heart once again.

Renew a spirit of honesty and integrity in me, Lord. I know how precious I am to You. Don't let me waste that kind of love on trivial pursuits or quests that end in heartbreak. My life is transformed when this internal renewal takes place. Such a miracle can happen only with Your power and grace.

Timeless Beauty

He saved us through the washing of rebirth and renewal by the Holy Spirit, whom he poured out on us generously through Jesus Christ our Savior, so that, having been justified by his grace, we might become heirs having the hope of eternal life.

—TITUS 3:5-7

Baptized in Your Spirit, Lord, I walk through my life as a new creation—a woman reborn into a life measured by her Creator's love. When I feel run-down or unable to move forward through the daily grind, I reflect on this spiritual act of rebirth and am instantly lifted above earthly concerns.

Women everywhere strive for perfection, timeless beauty, and a renewed physical package. Meanwhile they ignore inner flaws of doubt, worthlessness, and envy. May I never exchange Your hope for false securities. May I never trade the desire for spiritual perfection for the pursuit of physical improvement. My hope is placed in the only timeless beauty: eternal life.

Foot in Mouth

Lord, I have heard of your fame; I stand in awe of your deeds, O Lord. Renew them in our day, in our time make them known.

—HABAKKUK 3:2

"Show them, God!" Sometimes I scream this in my mind when standing around people with hardened hearts who do not understand the essence of life and who work against goodness. I call out to You like You are Superman. Save them. Save us. Save me.

You are all-powerful, Lord, so show them. Show these people who do not know pure love and forgiveness what Your grace is all about. Change the hearts of those who have bad intentions and who are self-destructive. I have read biblical accounts of Your influential appearances. Why not renew such deeds now? I want *my* peers, *my* culture to sense Your might.

This is when You return my command back to me, and I am humbled. Hear my new prayer today, Lord: "Help *me* show them You."

Plans

Making the Effort

Whatever your hand finds to do, do it with all your might, for in the grave, where you are going, there is neither working nor planning nor knowledge nor wisdom.

—ECCLESIASTES 9:10

This is my chance. I know this. I sometimes fixate on this fact. This is my one chance at life here on earth. You have given me this earthly body, this heart for You, and the plans You conceived for my life before it ever began. I pray that my efforts are worthy in Your sight, Lord. When I struggle and strain, let it be for a good cause. Let each and every effort I make be done with sincerity and honor.

Heaven's glory shimmers in the distance. I look toward it in my heart so I know the way home. But these days of living in full humanity also serve a divine purpose. I am to love You, love others, serve You, serve others, and discover who I am in the process.

Off Track

There is no wisdom, no insight, no plan that can succeed against the LORD.

—PROVERBS 21:30

I have a planner overflowing with...well, plans, of course. Each day's box lays claim to a portion of my life. I know that each time I set a commitment down in blue ink, I am also claiming a portion of the time You have planned for me. I imagine I am steering things in the wrong direction more times than not. I take great comfort in knowing You are able to guide my random efforts back to Your intention for my life.

As I make plans for the days ahead, may I seek Your guidance, Your priorities, and Your will. When I follow Your direction, the meaning of each day is magnified. The possibilities to serve You become clear.

Forever Heart

*But the plans of the LORD stand firm forever, the
purposes of his heart through all generations.*

—PSALM 33:11

Lord, I spend most of my time pursuing goals and
dreams that are temporal. Maybe that is the hardest part
about being human—knowing that the future dreams I
have might not come to fruition. There is an expiration
date on my life and these dreams.

When I turn to Your plan for eternal life, I face a
lasting hope. The purposes of Your heart have accom-
panied generations before me, and they will carry
future generations heavenward. I hold tightly to Your
promises and know they will live on when my other
dreams have faded. It is a wonderful gift You give
me...something to believe in...a dream come true.

The First Step

*In his heart a man plans his course, but the L*ORD *determines his steps.*

—PROVERBS 16:9

I have great intentions, Lord. You know my heart carries with it many hopes and plans. Some have come to pass, and others I wait for with patience from You. But lately I sense my life shifting ever so slightly. One moment, my eyes are cast on a defined horizon, and in the next, they are peering at something hazy. Without my permission, without my foreknowledge, my true future emerges. You encourage my spirit to carry on.

Thank You, God, for letting me rest in the security of Your plans, not my own. Things change—sometimes so quickly that I lose my footing. But as I take the first step in a new direction, I know You are holding me upright and directing each step.

Grace

Overflowing

From the fullness of his grace we have all received
one blessing after another.

—JOHN 1:16

I have been filled with pride, overflowing with love; consumed by longing, brimming with gratitude. Want leaves me empty of satisfaction. Excess leaves me bloated with regret. So why does my heart ride the chaotic range of these two extremes when I have You? Surely I have learned that nothing satisfies like the fullness of Your grace.

For too long, my God, I have stepped over and on blessings as I make my way to prayers for more blessings. Please show me all the riches in my life that come directly from Your hand. Remove from my spirit any longing, sin, preoccupation; the space they leave behind is meant for Your fulfillment, grace, and will. Empty me. Fill me.

Reality Check

For by the grace given me I say to every one of you: Do not think of yourself more highly than you ought, but rather think of yourself with sober judgment, in accordance with the measure of faith God has given you.

—ROMANS 12:3

Lord, I thank You for recent successes in my life. I have a sense of independence that is very fulfilling. But I know I am where I am because of Your grace. When I face moments of true satisfaction and bring my warm, fuzzy self-love into the light, I will realize how many cracks, stains, and faults this human vessel has. Reality checks are healthy. I want to turn my loving gaze back to You.

Lord, I am in awe of You. I pray that any step forward I make will be done with Your guidance. Your grace allows me the freedom to get caught up in myself. And Your grace allows me to return to You…dependent, thankful, and so full of love for my Savior.

Wherever I Go

The grace of the Lord Jesus Christ be with your spirit. Amen.

—PHILIPPIANS 4:23

Wherever I go, Your grace goes with me. I cannot be hidden from grace because it is within my spirit. You could have kept such a hold on Your gift, Lord, allotting it to those who are deserving on a daily basis. Instead, You fill our spirits with Your forgiveness and mercy. The world does not offer me security. I find it only in You.

I give You my actions today, Lord. I want to reflect Your gift of grace through my words and deeds. I pray for those people I encounter throughout the day…may they come to know Your love and mercy. May I develop a heart of compassion that does not hesitate to extend grace to others.

Place of Grace

Let your conversation be always full of grace, seasoned with salt, so that you may know how to answer everyone.

—COLOSSIANS 4:6

Lord, I am often at a loss for words when talking to other people. In difficult situations of tension, grief, anger, or pain, I stumble through my thoughts and try to find something wise to hold on to...something worth sharing, something that is politically correct. I have forgotten to rely on the voice within that comes from You. As Your child, I can speak from a place of grace.

Lord, help me tap into Your love when I am searching for the "right" words. May I nourish other people's souls with a message from Your heart. And when I need encouragement, may I return to Your Word and immerse my mind and spirit in the language of grace.

Anticipation

But by Faith

*But by faith we eagerly await through the Spirit the
righteousness for which we hope.*

—GALATIANS 5:5

Patience is not one of my strengths, Lord. It is
a virtue I hope to develop as my faith grows and as
I understand my life in Your will. It is my faith that
enables me to wait at all. I impatiently wait for growth,
an answer, a sign, a finger coming out of the heavens
to point the way. Such a list!

Help me to rest in Your Spirit and in the faith I
have placed in You, my Lord. I pray for true righteousness—the kind that comes from perseverance. When I
am tested by trials and even doubt, may I be a woman
of conviction and commitment. You not only see me
through, but also carry me through these times. You
turn my times of waiting into moments of moving
forward.

Opening a Gift

So it is with you. Since you are eager to have spiritual gifts, try to excel in gifts that build up the church.

—1 CORINTHIANS 14:12

God, grant me spiritual gifts that serve Your body. In the past I have prayed for gifts that would help me succeed in different areas of my life. I wanted to give You glory, but I did not understand how the gifts I receive are meant to be given back to You and the family of believers.

The gifts You plant in my soul will emerge as I am ready to use them for good. May I never misinterpret Your blessings as permission to serve myself. While I anticipate the strengths You plan for my life, give me vision to recognize the spiritual gifts of other people so that I may encourage them and see You more clearly in the body of Christ.

Rushing to Do Good

Who is going to harm you if you are eager to do good?

—1 PETER 3:13

I can get ahead of myself when trying to do good. I anticipate the rewards of the situation. I see how one giving moment can turn a bad situation into a blessing. There is the power to change lives and hearts when I act on the impulse to serve You. Lord, direct these urges to do good so that I serve Your higher purpose and not my own.

You smile upon a child who desires to please You, who is eager to please her Father. Your love embraces me and holds me close to the security of Your mercy. How can I not be excited to share this comfort and holiness with other people? I hope You are proud of Your girl.

Waiting for Your Presence

I wait for you, O LORD; you will answer, O Lord my God.

—PSALM 38:15

My heart beats rapidly waiting for Your presence, Lord. I have called out to You in a moment of great need. I am so empty right now. I do not long for the conversation or advice of friends. I only want to be resting in Your hand. You know me so well. You see the places of my heart and my life that I hold back from the world, and You love me.

My lips form the name of my Savior because You are the sole Source of unconditional love. When I am emptied of energy and desire, I ask to be swept away to Your refuge. Just when I cannot be alone with my anxiety and humanity any longer, You answer my cries. Your mercy rushes over my worry and fills me with peace.

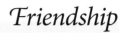

Friendship

A Friend's Prayer

My intercessor is my friend as my eyes pour out tears to God; on behalf of a man he pleads with God as a man pleads for his friend.

—JOB 16:20-21

My friend, who knows the Holy Spirit, prays for me, Lord. I am comforted by this knowledge. I can be tumbling headlong into a hectic day of work, and all of a sudden realize I have been bathed in prayer. I receive peace from the efforts of another.

My words to You come from my heart and are meaningful through the Spirit's interpretation. Yet, I find a deeper comfort knowing that a friend lifts up words to Your ears. She calls upon the Holy Spirit to hear her pleas on my behalf. I have a friend who knows Jesus, and we both have a friend in You. Thank You, Lord.

Friends in High Places

I am a friend to all who fear you, to all who follow your precepts.

—PSALM 119:63

There was a time when I followed the steps of those who did not care about Your existence. I emulated their mannerisms, which reflected worldly poise. I am thankful I woke up from this false dream. When I noticed You on the perimeter of life, I knew right away that I had set my sights too low for myself. There was something greater...no, Someone greater to follow.

I thank You for bringing godly people into my life. My path is not always straight. I wander. I take long detours that should be day trips. My friends who know You and fear You with their every breath give me directions back to Your way. They stay true to Your precepts; You stay true to me.

Misplaced Friendship

Anyone who chooses to be a friend of the world becomes an enemy of God.

—JAMES 4:4

Forgive me, Lord, for the times when I choose the world over You. With all You have done for me, I cannot believe I am still tempted by the world. Yet I am. I think it relates to my insecurities. The times when I do not trust You are the times when someone else's success or position in life has influence over my heart.

Recently, I have felt a need to be accepted by the world. Forgive me for leaning toward the artificial light of the world when I have the brilliance of Your glory in my heart. The trivial needs will pass, and I will be left with truth—Your truth. Lead me back to You, Lord. I do not want any part of me to flow against Your will...even my longings.

Making a Connection

*If one falls down, his friend can help him up. But pity
the man who falls and has no one to help him up!*

—ECCLESIASTES 4:10

I have a full life: family, work, church, commitments. But I am missing the connection of a close
friend. I have had that in my life, so I understand
what is lacking. I turn to You with my concerns and
my joys, Lord, just as I should. But I need a friend of
the flesh, who experiences the trials of life as I do. You
know my heart intimately. Now I want to share it with
a special friend.

Please let me be open to whom this friend might
be. Perhaps it is someone already in my life. Maybe
You are directing a stranger to cross paths with me.
Let my judgment be put aside. I don't want to miss the
chance to connect with someone You have chosen for
me. I believe friendships lead us to a deeper relationship with You. I cannot wait to meet the special friend
You have for me.

Responsibility

The Greater Good

For it is God who works in you to will and to act according to his good purpose.

—PHILIPPIANS 2:13

The other day I felt You move within me. I was ready to denounce my responsibility. I was ready to distance myself from a commitment. And You prodded my soul to act wisely and in a godly way. I didn't fully understand it at the time, but I see now that You were leading me toward a higher purpose.

Just when I think all circumstances come down to what I want versus what other people want, You step in and remind me that there is indeed a good purpose to be fulfilled. I thank You for this new perspective. May I be aware of how the greater purpose affects the faith of those around me. Work in me. Work through me. Lord, use me as You wish.

Remaining

Brothers, each man, as responsible to God, should remain in the situation God called him to.

—1 CORINTHIANS 7:24

I want to shed my current situation. But I know You have called me to be here. This "now" I am experiencing is within Your will. I sense that when I pray for release. You ask me to be patient, willing, and open.

I am overwhelmed by responsibilities I juggle in life. Ordering their priority is not simple. Help me realize that I don't have to understand how all these pieces fit together in a master plan. My only responsibility is to You. My commitment to rest in my current situation is an act of faith. I follow Your call and hold onto the hope of things to come.

Working Toward Maturity

Perseverance must finish its work so that you may be mature and complete, not lacking anything.

—JAMES 1:4

That problem I neglected to give over to You has circled back to me again. While I did not bring it to You, I did toss it into the cosmos, and I thought it would sort of drift forever. Well, it is here now for a return engagement. Lord, help me give this to You once and for all. Then give me strength to learn the lesson of perseverance.

I require so much work, Lord, and yet You continue to provide me with what I need, when I need it. I never lack for anything. I am grateful for the times when You called me to wait, to learn, to push through a situation. You patiently work in my life so that I may become complete in You.

Strength in Obedience

She sets about her work vigorously; her arms are strong for her tasks.

—PROVERBS 31:17

God, let me dive into the tasks I have before me at work and at home. I want to face my responsibilities with great strength and effort. I want to be hardworking in every setting. May my focus be to serve You, no matter what the job. When I honor You with the labor of my hands and mind, I know it strengthens me spiritually. Everything is connected to what is good and right.

Lead me to responsibilities that are of importance to You. Guide me away from fruitless efforts. I want my life to count. I want my work to please You.

Place

Creating an Altar

When they reached the place God had told him about, Abraham built an altar there and arranged the wood on it.

—GENESIS 22:9

Lord, I am ready to build a place of sacrifice for You. I believe my pursuit of many personal objectives has kept me from creating an altar for You in my life. How do I begin? What obstacles must first be torn down to make room? I have much debris to clear from my mind and heart, but I am ready for this to be done.

When the altar of faith is built, Lord, is my heart the only sacrifice I must offer? Your Son died on the cross and rose three days later so I would not have to build physical altars. Love replaced the law of such a process. Yet, You do call me to make my life a living sacrifice to You. I bring to You my every waking moment, I give You my dreams, and I give You my days. Please accept this offering.

God's Dwelling Place

I will put my dwelling place among you, and I will not abhor you. I will walk among you and be your God, and you will be my people.

—LEVITICUS 26:11-12

You are a God who does not reign from a mighty throne in a distant land. From the beginning, You wanted to be a God of relationship and love. You spoke to the leaders whom You formed from dust. You parted the seas. You moved the earth. You continue to work in mighty ways. As a believer, there is no denying how You have changed my life.

Even with all Your power, You still choose to dwell within the hearts of Your children. You guide by the Spirit, and Your love and strength are amazingly accessible. Create Your place in my heart, Lord. I want to be filled by Your presence and be counted among Your people.

Land of My Future

*Now Moses said to Hobab son of Reuel the Midianite,
Moses' father-in-law, "We are setting out for the
place about which the LORD said, 'I will give it to
you.' Come with us and we will treat you well, for
the LORD has promised good things to Israel."*

—NUMBERS 10:29

Like a child staring at a wrapped birthday present,
I cannot wait to open the gift You have for me. You
have given me a place in the future, a place that is my
future. When troubles pull me away from hope, I look
to the land ahead and imagine the blessings You have
planted for my harvest.

I do not know how You will shape my later days,
but I do know I will never claim the goodness ahead
unless today involves a step forward in Your will.
You speak to my heart of promises yet to be fulfilled
in my life. I look ahead with expectation and belief.
As I move ahead, place to place, my love for You
grows—not because You give a gift, but because You
remember me.

Refuge

You are my hiding place; you will protect me from trouble and surround me with songs of deliverance.

—PSALM 32:7

Faced with fear, I go inside myself. Emotionally I curl up so small that any threatening trouble will overlook me and continue on its way. I reach for other people, Lord, but for true comfort and peace I prefer Your presence. Your stillness inside my heart shames away boisterous difficulties. Harm cannot come to me here. You never said You would remove trials for Your children. You offer something better: a place of rescue.

Save me, Lord, from the loneliness of this particular struggle. Once my strength is restored, I will return to the daily clatter. Right now, though, it does my soul good to listen to the melodic voice of my Deliverer.

Longing

Longing for Company

*And now, O Israel, what does the LORD your God
ask of you but to fear the LORD your God, to walk
in all his ways, to love him, to serve the LORD your
God with all your heart and with all your soul, and
to observe the LORD's commands and decrees that I
am giving you today for your own good?*

—DEUTERONOMY 10:12-13

When was the last time I spoke to You from my
heart? Some days bring trials, others bring joy. Today
brings a mixture of both. I am thankful to have entered
into Your presence because I was longing for Your
company without even knowing it.

Is my day going as You planned? Am I missing
something wonderful, important, divine? Help me
embrace today's complexities, questions, and ordinary
demands. Somehow just sitting here in Your presence
is changing my outlook for the rest of today. Did You
need to remind me that You were walking beside me?
My pace has been so fast, sometimes even reckless,
that I forgot how steady a moment can be. With just
a brush of Your Spirit, my day has taken on the color
of hope.

Waiting to Talk

You will call and I will answer you; you will long for
the creature your hands have made.

—JOB 14:15

I have allowed days and days to go by without talking to You, Lord. In fact, a whole season of life seems to have blurred by while I tapped my fingers and waited for change, peace, better things. Why in a time of drought do I forget to pray for rain? I have failed to keep up my end of the dialogue in the past, and You have been faithful. I suppose it is because You have not left. You wait. You move in and through my life and wait for me to respond.

So I call to You today, Lord. On my knees I bow before You and pray for You to hear me. Before Your presence covers me, I taste the dryness of desperate longing. I understand what it means to wait for a response from someone I love.

Savoring

A longing fulfilled is sweet to the soul, but fools detest turning from evil.

—PROVERBS 13:19

"Be careful what you wish for." Oh, the wise sayings of man! But it is true. The rush of claiming an object of longing pushes aside any thought of consequences. I know I set my sights on desires that are not of You. But the pursuit can be sweet nonetheless. Lord, help me see how these worldly prizes are empty.

Turn my eyes and spirit from the road leading to ruin. Set my path in the right direction. Give my heart a passion for Your knowledge, grace, and love. When earthly longings enter my field of vision, let me see them for what they are: distractions. Let nothing keep me from absolute fulfillment in You. Let me savor Your sweetness.

A Better Country

They were longing for a better country—a heavenly one. Therefore God is not ashamed to be called their God, for he has prepared a city for them.

—HEBREWS 11:16

My days have been crazy, God. I want to abandon my life right now and give it to You with instructions to fix it all. Some choices of mine have complicated matters. My inability to say no to requests for time and energy is now binding my feet and hands. I cannot move toward any greater purpose until I am freed.

So give me clarity today, Lord. Tell me which way to go, how to say no, when to say yes. As Your child I long for the days of heaven's glory and ease. Oh, how I hope there is ease. Meanwhile, I hold on to You and ask You to lead me through this life until I can come home.

Becoming

Purpose

The LORD will fulfill his purpose for me; your love,
O LORD, endures forever—do not abandon the works
of your hands.

—PSALM 138:8

Will I ever feel as though I have arrived? When I was a child I could not wait until adulthood. I thought all the mysteries of life would become known. And I was certain a sense of deliberate purpose would fill me. I am still not at this place of understanding, Lord. But I do know Your love.

Lord, work out Your will in me and through me. Make my days fruitful. Guide me in my choices and in my attitude as I become the person You created me to be. Let me carry on with purpose, trusting in Your love.

Stay or Go

In him we were also chosen, having been predestined according to the plan of him who works out everything in conformity with the purpose of his will, in order that we, who were the first to hope in Christ, might be for the praise of his glory.

—EPHESIANS 1:11-12

As I question my current direction in life, Lord, I ask You to shine Your light on the way I am to go. If I am on track, I need to stop doubting my circumstances just because I am not fulfilled. I will not have an excuse to wallow in self pity any longer. I promise to keep on the path You give me.

As a chosen child of Yours, I know You care about every step I take. My direction does matter. And my fulfillment directly relates to Your higher purpose for my life. Let me rest in Your love and Your proven faithfulness. If this direction is the right one, then I sing Your praises, Lord. Let me know, Lord: Do I stay or go?

Become Wise

Take heed, you senseless ones among the people; you
fools, when will you become wise?

—PSALM 94:8

Just when I am really confident in myself and my
abilities, I realize that I get through my busy days
relying mainly on wit, quick thinking, and sarcasm.
At best, my skill involves strategic decision-making.
But, Lord, I need Your wisdom. Life presents so many
baffling changes and circumstances that my foolish,
just-getting-by ways present me with little comfort
and guidance.

Lead me in the ways of wisdom. I want to be Your
pupil, Lord. I will turn to Your Word and will seek Your
face as I strive to leave foolishness behind.

Transformed

And we eagerly await a Savior from there, the Lord Jesus Christ, who, by the power that enables him to bring everything under his control, will transform our lowly bodies so that they will be like his glorious body.

—PHILIPPIANS 3:20-21

Heaven is the place where we become complete. You will transform our lowly bodies into beautiful reflections of Your glory. Nothing will be as it is now. I am glad I do not know much about heaven, Lord. I believe that my earthly perspective would lessen the wonders of what You have prepared for Your children.

In Your presence, sickness becomes health, anger becomes joy, doubt becomes certainty, and fear becomes peace. I cannot wait to become one of the living...the eternal living.

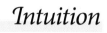

Intuition

The Seeing Blind

*Like the blind we grope along the wall, feeling our
way like men without eyes.*

—ISAIAH 59:10

When I am not tapped into the Spirit, I let demands,
schedules, and requests direct my steps. I grasp
for anything that appears to be stable but am often
deceived. Help me reach out for You as I stumble
along.

Let me draw on the wisdom of Your Spirit. I want
to rely on Your truth to lead me forward. I do not want
to walk like a blind man, when I have been given Your
gift of sight through Your leading. May I be strong
enough to resist the pull of the world's demands and
walk straight and steady.

A Vessel for Truth

We have not received the spirit of the world but the Spirit who is from God, that we may understand what God has freely given us. This is what we speak, not in words taught us by human wisdom but in words taught by the Spirit, expressing spiritual truths in spiritual words.

—1 CORINTHIANS 2:12-13

Lord, give me the words to say to other people. Let me speak from the Spirit to encourage them, lead them, and direct them to faith. You give me the Spirit freely. May I draw upon this source of strength and peace at all times. My joys will brighten; my sorrows will lighten.

I praise You, my Creator and Redeemer, for You are worthy of praise. I long to become a vessel for Your spiritual truths. May these truths flow through me in words of wisdom. I rest in the peace growing stronger within me every day.

Tap into the Gift

Let the word of Christ dwell in you richly as you teach and admonish one another with all wisdom, and as you sing psalms, hymns and spiritual songs with gratitude in your hearts to God.

—COLOSSIANS 3:16

You are my hiding place, Lord. You also dwell within my spirit. When I live on the surface and ride the wave of materialism, I miss out on using the gift of Your inner teachings. I want my wisdom to be based on Your truth. I want to share with other people without a sense of personal importance. Use me, my Lord. Strip me of my self-dependence, and cause me to rely solely on You.

I have such gratitude in my heart because of Your goodness. I want my soul to be a place that welcomes grace and returns it to the world through kindness and compassion. Let my song of living ring with truth and resound within the hearts of other people.

Bad Influences

Do not be misled: "Bad company corrupts good character." Come back to your senses as you ought, and stop sinning; for there are some who are ignorant of God—I say this to your shame.

—1 CORINTHIANS 15:33-34

I should have trusted the still, small voice within today. I felt it even before I heard it. Then I coughed to drown out the sound, made a commotion to distract my spirit, and headed into the fray of a bad day—a bad day that just got worse. I participated in gossip; I let negativity override a sense of accomplishment; I pretended I was responsible for my own worth.

Lord, keep me from the bad influence of other people on my life. While it might continue, may I resist the urge to give myself over to false praise, pride, and words that tear down other people. My heart is better than that because it is Yours. I will honor You with a better effort tomorrow, Lord. I promise to let that inner voice speak to my life.

Charity

Lending a Hand

She opens her arms to the poor and extends her hands to the needy.

—PROVERBS 31:20

To whom should I give today? Whom can I help? Let me start the day with this question, Lord. If I am asking to be of service, then I cannot ignore the opportunities when they arise. I have looked into needy faces and kept walking. I think too much about such things. My mind asks, "How can I fix someone's life?"

You ask me to be a woman of charity and kindness. My actions to assist another child of God become a part of Your will for that person. You are not calling me to fix her, to make her whole. Only You can do that. My job is to lend a hand along the way.

The Riches of Hope

Command those who are rich in this present world not to be arrogant nor to put their hope in wealth, which is so uncertain, but to put their hope in God, who richly provides us with everything for our enjoyment. Command them to do good, to be rich in good deeds, and to be generous and willing to share.

—1 TIMOTHY 6:17-18

You are my Provider, Lord. You gave me life, and You will create ways for me to follow in Your way. I should not question this, yet I have been in situations where financial uncertainty caused me to doubt the plans You have for me. I question what tomorrow might bring, rather than counting on what my Lord might bring.

I turn my circumstances over to You today. I will accept the goodness and the riches You allow. From the blessings You give, I will give to other people. I will strive to put my hope in You, God, not in my bank account. Let this step of faith encourage me to take bigger leaps tomorrow.

All Blessings Flow

You will be made rich in every way so that you can be generous on every occasion, and through us your generosity will result in thanksgiving to God.

—2 CORINTHIANS 9:11

The riches I can claim are Yours. They should flow through me and on to other people as You see fit. Lord, help me work through the urge to hold on to wealth. My fear of the future and my perceived need turn my willingness into reluctance. Keep me from blocking the blessings You have for other people.

Give me personal contact with those who need provision, or let me hear of a specific need I can help fill. My obedience can turn another person's cry for help into songs of thanksgiving.

Pure Refreshment

A generous man will prosper; he who refreshes others will himself be refreshed.

—PROVERBS 11:25

God, I have so much. Show me how to share the nonmonetary blessings I have: family, health, opportunity, stability, shelter, friends. Maybe I could invite someone to a family gathering during the holidays. I could encourage a friend with handwritten notes. I could use my health and participate in a fund-raiser walk. There are so many ways for me to extend Your provision to other people.

Refresh me, Lord. Fill me with the joy of giving. And let each offering refresh the spirit of another.

Peace

The Way of Peace

*The way of peace they do not know; there is no
justice in their paths. They have turned them into
crooked roads; no one who walks in them will know
peace.*

—ISAIAH 59:8

Lord, correct my ways when I am walking a
crooked road. I know the pain that consumes people on
roads paved with regret, anger, or resentment. There is
no peace along this path. When I turn my eyes to You,
I move toward freedom. The chains that shackle me to
past mistakes are removed only by Your power.

Present me with life lessons that redirect me and
propel me forward in Your will. God, guide me back
to Your grace. It is the way to peace. I know that in
Your goodness You will honor this prayer, because that
is the way of peace.

A Place of Peace

"The glory of this present house will be greater than the glory of the former house," says the LORD *Almighty. "And in this place I will grant peace," declares the* LORD *Almighty.*

—HAGGAI 2:9

This time in my life is not like any other time before. This place along my journey will be greater than any other because I know You better. I have held onto You through the difficulties and the delights. You have carried me from past times of trial into present times of peace.

While I have sought peace from other sources, I knew they were temporary solutions for eternal needs. That is never a match. But when I discovered You, I began a journey to a new place—a place of hope and promise that rests in Your embrace.

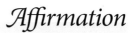

Affirmation

Yesterday Offers Faith for Today

O LORD, God of Israel, there is no God like you in heaven above or on earth below—you who keep your covenant of love with your servants who continue wholeheartedly in your way. You have kept your promise to your servant David my father; with your mouth you have promised and with your hand you have fulfilled it—as it is today.

—1 KINGS 8:23-24

Lord, your faithfulness is so evident when I look at my life today. I still have my list of things I want to achieve or of the flaws I hope to turn over to You, but just look at how far I have come. When I look back on my past struggles, I see how You lifted me out of my trench of doubt. You told me I mattered because I was Your own. You also didn't let me settle, when settling seemed so acceptable. I just wanted a little bit of relief, and You were offering complete healing. How limited my perspective is!

Today affirms all that I know about You, because in the clarity of hindsight there is not a bit of doubt. May my today be a testimony to Your grace, which is so evident when I survey my yesterdays.

Power in the Message

But they did not believe the women, because their words seemed to them like nonsense.

—LUKE 24:11

When people question my message of Your grace, they call my words nonsense. They are ignoring the possibility of miracles in their own lives, and it saddens me. I can only imagine how it saddens Your heart. Sometimes my words are discarded before their meaning can be taken in…because I am a woman.

I am made in Your image. I carry in my heart a secret that is meant to be shared. Your love overcomes the deafness of ignorance, so I will continue to share the good news. And when my gender or my presentation of Your message causes it to be written off as nonsense, I will stand tall in Your confidence in me and keep on trying.

Resting in Confidence

His master replied, "Well done, good and faithful servant! You have been faithful with a few things; I will put you in charge of many things. Come and share your master's happiness!"

—MATTHEW 25:23

I thank You for the many things on my plate right now. I am able to help people. I work to create a good home. I serve You and Your church with my gifts. You are so faithful, Lord. You have affirmed me and my current direction by blessing me with worthwhile responsibilities and opportunities.

I am finding fulfillment, thanks to Your guidance. I am more certain of myself, and my confidence in You grows with each passing day. When I finish a busy day and feel good, strong, and peaceful, I sense Your reassuring words: "Well done."

Just Ask and Believe

If you believe, you will receive whatever you ask for in prayer.

—MATTHEW 21:22

I believe. I do, Lord. And I have a whole list of things to ask for. Lately I have been slack in numerous areas. It is because I let insecurities take over my identity in You. What a shame that is! All I need to do is ask You for guidance, perseverance, wisdom, and peace for my circumstances. You affirm my faith when You answer such prayers.

In the days ahead I will look for greater confidence and security to replace my weaknesses. I will watch for evidence of Your power in my life. I have been here before and know of Your faithfulness. As Your promises unfold, the glory will be Yours.

Truth

Show Me

*I have chosen the way of truth; I have set my heart
on your laws.*

—PSALM 119:30

I am so thankful I discovered truth when I did.
I was all over the place seeking answers to random
questions. I didn't even know what to ask in my quest
for understanding and identity. You raised me out of
my ignorance and showed me the light of Your heart.
Everything clicked at that moment.

I still have times of confusion. I still have obstacles
to overcome, but never without a measure of truth to
guide me. Now my many questions are replaced by
one request: Show me the way, Lord.

Absolutes

We know also that the Son of God has come and has given us understanding, so that we may know him who is true. And we are in him who is true—even in his Son Jesus Christ. He is the true God and eternal life.

—1 JOHN 5:20

Lord, do you see all the ways women are invited to falseness? A pretentious attitude and a modified appearance will get you far. That is what the world offers. No wonder so many women and young girls struggle with a sense of self. Your love grounds Your children in truth about their worth. We are all valuable because we are Yours.

Even if I cannot always tell which world image is real or retouched, I know the image of the cross is true. I can believe in You completely.

Words of Truth

Jesus answered, "I am the way and the truth and the life. No one comes to the Father except through me. If you really knew me, you would know my Father as well. From now on, you do know him and have seen him."

—JOHN 14:6-7

To be able to see You, Lord, is a blessing. Reading Your Word provides me with a picture of Your character, Your nature, Your love. While faith can be defined as belief in something unseen, my faith in You goes beyond that. I do see You. In the beauty of the earth, in the smile of a child, and in each victory of justice, I see Your face.

Each day I try to know Christ better. It is my way to move closer to the truth of creation and the truth of eternity. I am stronger than ever before because I follow this quest for a deeper understanding of You and Your Son.

Self-Deception

If we claim to be without sin, we deceive ourselves
and the truth is not in us.

—1 JOHN 1:8

To maintain my sense of status in the world, I sometimes build myself up with half-truths. I have moments
when I would rather believe lies than seek Your truth.
I am weak in that way. But the bottom always falls out
from beneath plans based in deception. Sooner or later
I end up back at the foot of the cross.

I have such sin, Lord. When I compare my human
fickleness to Your godly steadfastness, I am ashamed.
But there is redemption in faith that is grounded in Your
goodness. I return to You and Your unchanging truth.

Women

Sister Act

*Now, O women, hear the word of the LORD; open your
ears to the words of his mouth. Teach your daughters
how to wail; teach one another a lament.*

—JEREMIAH 9:20

Do I model Your love to other women, Lord? If
I could be an example to anyone, I would want to
show Your truth to women. Part of that truth relates
to the ability to tap into one's emotions. Contemporary
society requires such poise and control. We forget to
teach young women how important it is to feel grief
and pain fully. Difficult experiences bring us to Your
feet. They reveal Your mercy.

We grow strong only through our opportunities to
rely on You, Lord. My sense of ability comes only from
You. I desire to share with other women the security I
have found in my Savior. You are not only the epitome
of love, but the definition of love. Your love for each of
us is meant to be felt deeply.

Ask Father

Jesus answered her, "If you knew the gift of God and who it is that asks you for a drink, you would have asked him and he would have given you living water."

—JOHN 4:10

It took me a long time to drink from the living water. I felt Your presence before but chose to ignore Your offer of salvation. I think of the many bright, accomplished women who do not know You. On the world's terms, they might seem to be filled with truth and knowledge, but I know You have much more planned for their lives.

God, I pray for women who do not yet call You by name. I pray for the women who see a father figure as someone who is abusive or critical or unloving. Let them embrace the Father that I know so dearly and truly. Show them the true, loving image of the Savior.

Keep Talking

*The angel said to the women, "Do not be afraid,
for I know that you are looking for Jesus, who was
crucified. He is not here; he has risen, just as he
said. Come and see the place where he lay. Then go
quickly and tell his disciples: 'He has risen from the
dead and is going ahead of you into Galilee. There
you will see him.' Now I have told you."*

—MATTHEW 28:5-7

You give me a wonderful message to share, Lord.
You entrust me with a mighty word to speak to other
people. My personal testimony is not elaborate, but it
contains the miracle of spiritual rebirth.

You revealed Your resurrection to women, and Your
angel directed them to share the news. I believe You
continue to use women in this way. Your goodness is
for every one of Your children. May I follow in the
footsteps of those who loved You when You walked
the earth. And may I continue to believe the wonder I
have been shown: Your love.

You Call Me Daughter

Jesus turned and saw her. "Take heart, daughter," he said, "your faith has healed you." And the woman was healed from that moment.

—MATTHEW 9:22

Lord, I have shed tears over a particular hurt in my life. Though it is not a recent wound, it reopens when I am most fragile. Like many women, I let the daily stresses distract me from the pain, but eventually the heart and mind return to the source of anxiety. Forgive me, Father, for holding this sorrow within my soul, for thinking I could fix it on my own.

This wound never mended because I have never reached out in desperation to You. I wanted control over my hurts. I was ashamed to come to You. But today my faith leads me to You. I reach for the hem of Your robe and believe. And You heal Your daughter once and for all.

Relationships

A Worthy Friend

Likewise, teach the older women to be reverent in the way they live, not to be slanderers or addicted to much wine, but to teach what is good. Then they can train the younger women to love their husbands and children, to be self-controlled and pure, to be busy at home, to be kind, and to be subject to their husbands, so that no one will malign the word of God.

—TITUS 2:3-5

I thank You for the relationships I have with other women. Some have already walked through the experiences I am having. Their shared wisdom encourages me to keep going, to take a new look at my situation, to be thankful for the process of living. My kinship with younger women is also very fulfilling. I understand the role I can play as mentor, friend, confidante, and prayer partner.

Lord, in all my relationships with women, help me to be a good friend who reflects grace, not judgment; who offers support, not competition; who gives hope, not anxiety.

It Is Personal

*For your Maker is your husband—the L*ORD
Almighty is his name—the Holy One of Israel is your
Redeemer; he is called the God of all the earth.

—ISAIAH 54:5

You are the love of my life. You are the Lord of my life. You care for and nourish my soul because You created it with all of its needs, intricacies, and mysteries. The times when other people let me down, or when I let myself down, You lifted me up on wings of Your faithfulness.

Some days I do not know myself well. I question my actions and my direction. My comfort is in You. You speak to the depths of my being and remind me that I am Yours, and that is all that matters. You are called the God of all the earth, and You have a personal relationship with me. Thank You, Lord.

Serving One Another

However, each one of you also must love his wife as he loves himself, and the wife must respect her husband.

—EPHESIANS 5:33

Marriage is a precious gift. God, please watch over my marriage relationship. Help me respect the dreams and choices of my husband. Guide him to love and cherish me as we work together toward our future. I pray that we will always rely on You for guidance and direction.

Let us follow Your example of unconditional love as we care for one another. God, reveal to us the ways we can serve one another as we also serve You.

Love One Another

Dear friends, let us love one another, for love comes from God.

—1 JOHN 4:7

My love comes with limits. I didn't learn that from You, Lord, so why does my heart restrict its capacity to love other people? When I am afraid of commitment, please give me peace to move forward. If I feel I do not have enough love to extend to another person, please urge me to trust Your command to love one another.

Love comes directly from You. Let me receive it with grace and give it with peace.

Freedom

Like No Other

I will walk about in freedom, for I have sought out your precepts.

—PSALM 119:45

Trusting Your precepts offers me freedom in so many ways. I approach situations with confidence because I know Your leading is true. I arrange my priorities according to Your will. And I lean on Your understanding when life presents questions and difficulties.

Your Word sheds light on uncertain times. I am so grateful to call You "Lord" because there is power in Your name. Your gift of salvation releases me from the bondage of my sin; thank You for this freedom like no other.

Never Go Back

It is for freedom that Christ has set us free. Stand firm, then, and do not let yourselves be burdened again by a yoke of slavery.

—GALATIANS 5:1

God, You knew what it would take for us to be free from sin. And You sacrificed Your son. There is no way to repay such an act of sacrifice. I must honor Your amazing love by standing firm in Your freedom. I will not go back to a life of slavery. I will not let temptation lead me against the way of grace.

God, I humbly fall to my knees and praise You today. Show me where I am resisting Your freedom. Do not let me take advantage of Your mercy by resting in sin. I want to be holy and pleasing.

Without Condemnation

Jesus straightened up and asked her, "Woman, where are they? Has no one condemned you?" "No one, sir," she said. "Then neither do I condemn you," Jesus declared. "Go now and leave your life of sin."

—JOHN 8:10-11

When I stand beside You, Lord, Your grace covers me. Stones cannot be thrown at me in my state of sin because You protect me. Salvation frees me from this condemnation. Even as a saved child of God, I return to a life of sin. Not as before, but I have fallen on my way to good things. Yet You raise me up to stand beside You. Together we face my sin, and You cleanse me.

Lord, when my shame is unbearable, Your presence frees me to walk once more in grace.

Use It Well

Live as free men, but do not use your freedom as a cover-up for evil; live as servants of God.

—1 PETER 2:16

I have no excuse for my recent behavior, Lord. Under the guise of Christianity, I have behaved badly. I allowed grace in my life to become arrogance in my heart. I passed judgment on another person and laid claim to being right. My pride creates a mean spirit, when a situation truly calls for Your loving spirit.

I ask You to squelch this stubborn way in me, Lord. I do not serve You when my own objectives become priority. I do not want to be imprisoned by my sinful nature. Free me, Lord, to serve You well.

Speaking Up

Speak Up, Show Up

Speak up for those who cannot speak for themselves, for the rights of all who are destitute. Speak up and judge fairly; defend the rights of the poor and needy.

—PROVERBS 31:8-9

Lord, I pray for the many people who struggle to make ends meet: the families who face a life of shelters and job-searching, the mothers who care for their children and sacrifice their own health and well-being. Lord, pour out Your mercy on Your children living in poverty and fear of the future.

Help me reach out to ease the burden of another person. Am I looking closely at those people within my very reach? Who needs assistance? When I have so much, let me multiply the blessings You give to me by extending them to other people. Your plan is not for a few to prosper. Allow me the willingness to be a steward of kindness and wealth. It is all about speaking up and showing up for Your children in need.

The Power of God's Voice

Can you raise your voice to the clouds and cover yourself with a flood of water? Do you send the lightning bolts on their way? Do they report to you, "Here we are"?

—JOB 38:34-35

I can scream at tragedy, and it will not dissipate. I can shout at my wounds from past hurts, yet they will not heal. Lord, only when I call out to You, and You in turn speak to my life, can such things happen. My voice is meant to praise You; it is not meant to hold the power of God.

Lord, right now, my personal pain takes my breath away. I can only whisper to You. The words I lift up are praises. In the midst of my trial, praises bring me into Your presence. And there my soul is healed.

Wise Move

Does not wisdom call out? Does not understanding raise her voice?

—PROVERBS 8:1

I try to be a good leader, Lord. I seek Your assistance when faced with decisions, and I pray about my every step. Please let my words be filled with Your wisdom. It can be intimidating to lead other people when I do not have the right words and the right time.

When I turn to You before speaking out, You give me understanding. And wisdom calls out. I rely on You to be my voice. In my desire to lead, Lord, let my life be an expression of Your message of love.

Cry for Help

The righteous cry out, and the LORD hears them; he delivers them from all their troubles.

—PSALM 34:17

As I go about my day, I talk to You, Lord. You hear my every mumble. You pay attention to me even when I am ranting and raving. I ask for what I think I want. I insist that things change to suit my mood. Through it all, You still love me. You know I am finding my way.

Lord, forgive me when I bring You my troubles, yet neglect to say what is truly on my heart. Lord, I need You as desperately as I need air to breathe. Because You hear my cries, You turn lamentations into praises.

Holding On

Misplaced Trust

*You have let go of the commands of God and are
holding on to the traditions of men.*

—MARK 7:8

God, I want to resist the temptation to hold on to
the ways of mankind. Early in my faith, I reached for
and grasped Your teachings. I let them sink into my
spirit and fill me with knowledge and light. Now as I
ride the merry-go-round of life, I am tempted by the
brass rings of easy solutions. I reach for them instead
of Your precepts.

It is difficult to turn from old habits. I set my sights
on those who appear successful in life and try to follow
them. Help me release my grip on the world and its
truth, Lord. Inspire me to hold on to Your commands
with all my heart.

Reaching for Faith

Timothy, my son, I give you this instruction in keeping with the prophecies once made about you, so that by following them you may fight the good fight, holding on to faith and a good conscience.

—1 TIMOTHY 1:18-19

Lead me in Your instruction today, God. Let me clearly feel Your direction as I work and make choices. Maybe You will lead someone to speak words of truth into my life. I have received encouragement and wisdom through friends and even strangers in the past.

Do not let me feel alone in my efforts. Direct me toward the fellowship of other believers. Let them counsel me in Your way. I will hold on to my faith tightly today, Lord, and wait upon Your wisdom.

Letting Go of Nothing

Hold on to instruction, do not let it go; guard it well,
for it is your life.

—PROVERBS 4:13

When I filter out needless information from my gathering of knowledge, what remains are the eternal truths You provide. In my busyness, I acquire a lot of worthless detail about so many different things. I memorize addresses, PIN codes, passwords, airport regulations, and word processing shortcuts. There is little room left for Your instruction.

Clear my mind, Lord. Details are important, but when I come to You in prayer, I want to let go of these bits of nothingness. Let them fade away so I can hold tightly to Your instruction as You speak it into my heart.

The Strength of Jesus

But Christ is faithful as a son over God's house. And we are his house, if we hold on to our courage and the hope of which we boast.

—HEBREWS 3:6

"I am weak but He is strong." Yes, Jesus loves me. And I am so thankful. My weakness is more apparent all the time. I should be old enough to know better... about everything. But I don't. I take false steps in strange directions. I strive to measure up to the world's expectations. But what I really want is to measure up as a child of God who needs the help of her Lord. I want Your power in my life.

Help me turn my hope into true strength. I am weak. But I know the One who lifts me above my circumstances. Let courage grow from my active faith.

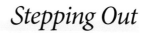

Stepping Out

A Confident Life

For God did not give us a spirit of timidity, but a spirit of power, of love and of self-discipline.

—2 TIMOTHY 1:7

When I approach situations that make me nervous, I focus on Your Spirit of power that resides within me. My timid days are behind me because I have Your strength as my foundation. Lord, give me a boldness I have never known. Let me step out with security in You.

Life will be new and different as I make decisions, communicate, and walk forward with this power. I will practice self-discipline and express love through my actions so that You, Lord, may use this new confidence for good.

Certainty

*Act with courage, and may the L*ORD *be with those who do well.*

—2 CHRONICLES 19:11

Fill me with courage, Lord. The confidence I receive from my worldly support is not strong. It wavers according to my current level of influence or popularity. It takes very little for my hopes to be dashed. I long to feel certain of myself and my life. I don't want opinions of other people to sway me from my known path.

I will keep my eyes upon You, Lord. Your love is my assurance. My faith and my salvation are certain. The confidence I have in these matters will lead to my success.

God Is with Me

Be strong and courageous, and do the work. Do not be afraid or discouraged, for the LORD God, my God, is with you.

—1 CHRONICLES 28:20

I think life is requiring too much work, Lord. I have tried all this time to be strong, but I am slipping backward. How can I keep up? Please help me continue through my trials when I don't have the energy to keep going. Break my stubborn spirit so I learn to lean upon Your strength.

I can do all things when I walk with You. I pray to be open to the work ahead. Let me not cower when You call on me to put forth great effort. It will not be unbearable. It will be the beginning of something miraculous.

Shine Forth

Commit your way to the Lord; trust in him and he will do this: He will make your righteousness shine like the dawn, the justice of your cause like the noonday sun.

—PSALM 37:5-6

Draw me to a life of commitment, Lord. Show me where I have sin that keeps me from embracing unconditional faith. I trust You with my eternity, so why is it difficult to turn over my here and now? Release me from fear and show me the life You have planned for me. I rise up and accept all that You are doing in my life.

Let my righteousness shine through even the darkest days. I will move forward as Your love warms me like the sun and prepares my heart for a great harvest.

Asking God

Praise

May my prayer be set before you like incense;
may the lifting up of my hands be like the evening
sacrifice.

—PSALM 141:2

I talk too much. My prayers don't leave room for breath and reflection. I petition without praise. Lord, lead me to a deeper prayer life. Even as I pray right now, I can let my mind wander to things that need to be done, or requests I want to make while I have Your attention.

Let me come to You in silence and with a spirit of worship. May my words wind their way to You like tendrils of burning incense. In Your presence I will surrender my own will.

Prayers of Protection

I have given them your word and the world has hated them, for they are not of the world any more than I am of the world. My prayer is not that you take them out of the world but that you protect them from the evil one.

—JOHN 17:14-15

I pray today as Your Son prayed for His followers. I ask for Your protection from evil while I am in the world. Being here creates opportunity for me to share my faith, to develop a deeper relationship with You, and to taste the richness of the life You have given me. But I know I am not truly of the world.

In troubled times I am tempted to ask You to remove my burdens or to release me from the pressure of life in the world. But You call me to walk in the plan You have for me. So protect me, Lord, for the rest of my days, so I can fulfill Your will.

Find Me Faithful

Be joyful in hope, patient in affliction, faithful in prayer. Share with God's people who are in need. Practice hospitality.

—ROMANS 12:12-13

May my life be a living prayer to You. When I cannot find the right words, let the beating of my heart do the speaking. May my actions toward other people be a prayer of hospitality and compassion. Lord, turn my fear into patience when I face hardship so I can demonstrate the power of prayer to other people.

Your Word reveals how to be a living prayer. I will glean from its endless wisdom and apply its truths to each situation. As long as there is need in my life and in the world, may You find me faithful in prayer and as a prayer.

Effective Prayer

And the prayer offered in faith will make the sick person well; the Lord will raise him up. If he has sinned, he will be forgiven. Therefore confess your sins to each other and pray for each other so that you may be healed. The prayer of a righteous man is powerful and effective.

—JAMES 5:15-16

Lord, I come to You today with my burden of sins. I hold each transgression up for a second look at my humanity. I place them in Your light for a closer look at Your grace. The practice of asking for forgiveness is important to my relationship with You. First, I am humbled and emptied of self. Then I am cleansed and filled with Your mercy.

When I pray, Lord, I know You hear me. I become vulnerable in Your presence because I have great faith in Your protection. May You call me righteous, and may my prayers be deemed powerful and effective.

Health

.

Healthy Soul

*Dear friend, I pray that you may enjoy good health
and that all may go well with you, even as your soul
is getting along well.*

—3 JOHN 2

I have noticed how my efforts toward a healthy life
have also enriched my soul. I am clear-thinking, brighter,
more attentive to my spiritual needs. Lord, I know I
complain about this body of mine, but I ask You to
bless it with healing and wholeness. Where I am having
physical difficulties, direct me toward the right care.
Don't let me abuse my body just because I am tired of
its shortcomings.

When I focus on my breath and think about the
oxygen soaring through my system, I am so grateful for
the intricate workings of my body. I was made by You,
and I will treat Your creation with kindness—inside
and out.

Healing Toward Peace

Nevertheless, I will bring health and healing to it; I will heal my people and will let them enjoy abundant peace and security.

—JEREMIAH 33:6

You heal. There is no other resource in my life that offers healing. You mend my brokenness with Your offer of wholeness. You remove the hurts I have been carrying around for years. Not only do You offer healing, but the new life I am given is one of abundance and great wonders.

You do not call my personal fulfillment trivial. Instead You guide me in a way that promises this fulfillment. I thank You, God, for being so gracious and giving.

Unhealthy Living

Because of your wrath there is no health in my body;
my bones have no soundness because of my sin.

—PSALM 38:3

My sin is like a wound. When left unattended, it becomes more painful, spreads, and deepens. The damage becomes more difficult to repair. But when I come to You right away, Lord, and confess my sin, the healing begins immediately. "Freedom from sin" is no longer just a phrase or bit of head knowledge. It is a real happening in my life. I actually have the sensation of a burden removed from my spirit.

Hear my prayers, Lord. Listen to my cries of repentance. Restore the strength of my flesh, bones, and soul.

Good to the Bone

A cheerful look brings joy to the heart, and good news gives health to the bones.

—PROVERBS 15:30

I need some good news about now, Lord. Recent days have been filled with sad news and frustrations. I haven't been able to focus and rarely get to bed on time. My spirit is restless. God, give me healing. From my flesh to my spirit, infuse my being with the power of Your good news.

I hold my faith close to me during this time. I take a walk outside and let nature's cheerfulness embrace me. Your presence is everywhere. You have not left me...even as I wait for good news and restoration.

Dancing

Recognizing the Time

There is a time for everything, and a season for every activity under heaven: ...a time to weep and a time to laugh, a time to mourn and a time to dance.

—ECCLESIASTES 3:1,4

You created a time for each season. You mastered a plan of cycles that allows endings and beginnings to flow together. Under heaven's gaze, I live through these seasons and try to adjust to them. Lord, I face a change right now and need to allow myself a chance to weep. As I face a transition, give me laughter so Your joy can touch my soul.

My time to mourn will be followed by chances to dance. I pray that Your presence will always be known in my life. May I never allow sadness to breed doubt when it is meant to breed hope for tomorrow.

Leaping for Joy

Then maidens will dance and be glad, young men and old as well. I will turn their mourning into gladness; I will give them comfort and joy instead of sorrow.

—JEREMIAH 31:13

God, thank You for releasing me from my painful experiences. The weight that pressed me down has been removed. Suddenly I want to dance. I want to leap with freedom. When I have seen the depths of mourning and Your hand still is able to pull me back to a place of peace, I have a new sense of what living is all about.

I bow to You and twirl across the days ahead. You are allowing me a second opportunity to feel deeply and to grow through sadness and blossom in shades of joy.

Sing unto the Lord

You turned my wailing into dancing; you removed my sackcloth and clothed me with joy, that my heart may sing to you and not be silent.

—PSALM 30:11-12

With all that You have going on, Lord, I am amazed that You still encourage my heart to express its emotions. One day I am asking for Your mercy. Another day I await Your blessing for an opportunity. You do not call me to be silent. While people rarely have time to hear the thoughts of another, You lovingly wait for my life song.

When my circumstances change, I owe it all to You. It is not of my doing that rain turns to sunshine. So it is not my doing when tears are dried by true joy. Thank You, Lord.

A New Dance

I will build you up again and you will be rebuilt, O Virgin Israel. Again you will take up your tambourines and go out to dance with the joyful.

—JEREMIAH 31:4

You are rebuilding me right now, Lord. I feel the growing pains. I see the unnecessary pieces of my life fall away. I watch as my new life emerges from the dust of construction. It is hard to be carved into a new being, Lord. Be gentle with me as You mold me into a creation that serves You even better.

There will be a day in the near future when I will dance. Music will flow through my life and give me a reason to shout with great happiness. God, please keep working on me. Your vision for my life is worth the wait.

Let It Be

Therefore do not worry about tomorrow, for tomorrow will worry about itself.

—MATTHEW 6:34

I want control over today and tomorrow. I know You can do a much better job, Lord, but I still battle for control. I don't have a great track record when I try to take the reins from Your hands. Let today affect my tomorrow. Give me the strength I need in this moment to give You my tomorrow.

There will be worries. There will be struggles. But tomorrow is also filled with possibility. I am inching closer to eternity, and this is a journey I want to savor, not suffer through. Give me the courage to live fully today and await tomorrow with great hope.

The
ONE-MINUTE PRAYERS™
Series

✐

One-Minute Prayers

One-Minute Prayers for Busy Moms

One-Minute Prayers for Healing

One-Minute Prayers for Men

One-Minute Prayers for Men Gift Edition

One-Minute Prayers for My Daughter

One-Minute Prayers for My Son

One-Minute Prayers for Singles

One-Minute Prayers for Those Who Hurt

One-Minute Prayers for Wives

One-Minute Prayers for Women

One-Minute Prayers for Women Gift Edition

One-Minute Prayers for Young Men

One-Minute Prayers for Young Women

One-Minute Prayers from the Bible

One-Minute Prayers to Begin and End Your Day

One-Minute Prayers to End Your Day

One-Minute Prayers to Start Your Day